Life
A Spiritual Pilgrimage

Nancy Drummond

insight *i* publishing group

Tulsa, Oklahoma

LIFE—A SPIRITUAL PILGRIMAGE

Life—A Spiritual Pilgrimage by Nancy Drummond
Published by Insight Publishing Group
8801 S. Yale, Suite 410
Tulsa, OK 74137
918-493-1718

ISBN 1-930027-62-1
Library of Congress catalog card number: 2002109797

Printed in the United States of America

Acknowledgments

Without the wonderful efforts of Lisa Lifgren, my daughter-in-law, Martha Bragg, my granddaughter, Carol Pearce, by daughter, and Susan Happel, a family friend, this project would not have been possible. Thank you!

"Life—A Spiritual Pilgrimage"

There would not have been a life, as I have known it, without Him. The Holy Eucharist, the Rosary, and my Catholic faith have all contributed to getting to know the Lord in an exciting, intimate way. He is my All. The stories I have presented in this book are part of my journey toward becoming united with Him. It is the road God has chosen for me. Hopefully, I have been listening and am an obedient servant. I feel He wishes me to share these thoughts and experiences with you. My hope is that this book will touch you, on some level, and allow you to understand the great love that God has for each one of us. Not just a general feeling of love, but an immense personal love, a longing to be one with us, to protect us, guide us, and eventually free us.

"With God There is a Way"

We were attending a lecture series given by several members of a religious group who were based in Nova Scotia. After they mentioned that they welcomed retreatants twelve months out of the year, my friend, who was seated next to me, exclaimed, "I would love to go for a week in the fall!" Immediately, I remarked that I might be interested in joining her.

In September, I wrote asking for a week's retreat in October and received a reply stating they had scheduled my **month's** retreat as requested. A month's retreat when I had asked for a week was a frightening thought. I could not visualize myself being absent from my family for such a long period of time. My youngest daughter Sarah, the only remaining child at home, was a high school student, and my husband, a pilot, traveled a great deal of the time. At morning Mass I asked God what He wanted me to do, and, "not" to my amazement, felt it was a "yes" to the month's retreat. God is full of surprises! If I am willing to say "Yes" when I am asked to do something which is beyond my wildest dreams, after the initial shock, comes peace! It turned out that my husband was home for most of the month and my friend decided not to accompany me!

Several weeks into my stay in Nova Scotia, I happened to ask one of the Sisters why they sent me a month when I asked only for a week. Her mouth dropped open and she exclaimed, "Oh, no!" I was then told that another lady named Nancy, also from Connecticut, had written at precisely the same time requesting a month's retreat. She had accidentally sent her the week and me the month. God is pretty sneaky! Later I was informed that the lady was going to get her month's retreat after all.

This same group was responsible for my trip to Calcutta. While on a retreat I met Kathy, a former nun of Mother Teresa's, who suddenly decided she wanted to go back to the Missionaries of Charity in Brooklyn and rejoin the Order. Just about the same time, I had received a letter from a friend in Connecticut who had been present in Kennedy Airport when Mother arrived from Calcutta. She wrote me about this exciting event. It was the only letter I received during the entire month of my stay in Nova Scotia. After sharing this with Kathy she became extremely enthusiastic about her old life and wished to accompany me back to the States. There was only one small problem. She had no money for an airline ticket and I didn't have enough cash to offer any assistance. Fortunately, money became available once the Sisters came forth with the announcement that I had overpaid them by $150. As a result, Kathy was able to return with me to Connecticut. From there, my husband and I drove her to her former residence in Brooklyn where Sister Nirmala was the superior in charge of Mother Teresa's contemplatives at that time. Through my meeting with Kathy, the ex-nun and consequently my contact with Sister Nirmala, our trip to Calcutta several years later became a reality. When I felt it was necessary to call India in order to reach Sister Nirmala, who had returned to Calcutta, Kathy was able to provide me with the phone number. Sister's reply to my question to whether we should come to India was, "Yes do come!" I felt as though God had issued an order!

My trip to India was subsidized by a distant relative's will. Since my husband had said that he was not willing to give me money to go to such a disease-ridden place, this money was essential. However, he liked and respected Sister Nirmala; therefore, he changed his mind concerning the trip after she encouraged us to come.

I discovered in November that a local church in town was having a pilgrimage to Our Lady of Guadalupe Shrine in celebration of her December Feast Day. When I called the travel agent to find out if it was possible for me to make a reservation, I was told that the quota for the trip was completely filled; however, if there were any cancellations she would get in touch with me immediately. The last week in November I received a phone call saying that one of the ladies who had signed up just informed them that her dog was expecting puppies and it was impossible for her to be away at that time. I had initally told the travel agent that I was not concerned about the trip, since I knew if God wanted me in Mexico, He would find a way—even if a lady's dog had to have puppies!

I received a brochure in the mail which described a pilgrimage to Poland. I happened to mention the upcoming trip to my husband. He strongly urged me to consider taking it. Since I had never thought of the possibility of going to Poland in the past, I was not overly enthusiastic about the prospect. However, after praying about it, I felt it was the right thing to do, and therefore, made my reservation.

While we waited in the airport for our departure, one of the ladies in the group announced she was looking forward to visiting Auschwitz the concentration camp. About six months prior to this trip, the thought had occurred to me that I must visit one of these camps some day. In fact, it was very important for me to do so. The fact that Auschwitz was in Poland had never crossed my mind.

Visiting Auschwitz was undoubtedly one of the highlights of my trip. What a revelation it was to discover there is a Hitler in all of us, particularly myself! Given the right circumstances and someone pushing the right button, we human beings are capable of incredible destruction. Mother Teresa once made this statement about herself. Here I am Lord! Do something with me!

"Love Conquers All"

God has shown me very clearly on many occasions that the only possible way I could accomplish what was being asked of me was to offer it as prayer for whomever He placed in my heart. It had to be for love of Him, my family, or for a particular individual whom He specifically brought to my attention.

Speight, my practical-minded husband, who had previously visited Fatima, presented me with a pair of kneepads before my first trip to the Shrine. Never did it occur to me that I would ever use them, but I put them in my luggage anyway just to please the man in my life.

While watching a film on Fatima the morning before our departure for the States, I suddenly felt God was asking me to put on those pads and walk the walk on my knees; a journey pilgrims take from one end of the piazza to the grotto where the Blessed Mother appeared. It was a pretty scary thought. Since I had observed pilgrims executing this maneuver during my visit, I did not wish to participate in this activity for one moment.

Around 4:30 p.m. I had no alternative but to give it my best try. After putting my kneepads on over my stockings, I slowly started to walk on my knees toward the Capelina. Only a short while later I knew the kneepads had to go, and without them, painfully continued my journey. A German lady approached me emphatically voicing her disapproval of my actions; however, her husband simply seemed embarrassed by his wife's behavior. To continue my walk had become very torturous, and the only way that I could do this at all was to offer up my discomfort for various individuals whom God put into my head to pray for. It made the action bearable, and even to a certain degree, enjoyable. As I took my last step, the bells in the church rang out the Ave Maria. It was a glorious experience. Sore, bloody knees were the result of this endeavor; however, God is wonderful! He never allowed me to experience difficulty sleeping that night or experience any discomfort on the plane while returning home the next day.

When I arrived back in Connecticut, I was informed that while I was praying on my knees for a certain friend in Fatima, Portugal, her husband's funeral was being held at the local church, Our Lady of Fatima. He had a fatal automobile accident while I was away. As the church bells in Fatima were chiming the Ave Maria, Father was singing this song as a closing hymn for the Mass. There is a six-hour difference between Wilton, Connecticut, and Fatima, Portugal, which made this possible. God's timing was perfect that day!

During the Thanksgiving holiday I accompanied my daughter, Carol, and her family to Medjugorje. Late one afternoon, Carol and I decided to climb the big mountain, Mt. Krizevac. I was freezing almost immediately after leaving our apartment. Fortunately, a woman walked towards us selling long underwear. She was a Polish lady trying to make some extra money for her stay in Medjugorje by peddling a few wares that she had in her possession. Those long snugglies were absolutely what I desperately needed, and my daughter likewise purchased some beautiful kitchen towels, which made wonderful Christmas gifts that year.

When we reached the bottom of the mountain we both knew that we had to attempt to climb this rocky path on our knees. Inch by inch we ascended to the Third Station of the Cross and then realized that it was not possible for us to continue any farther in this manner. There again, for me to be able to move one knee in front of the other, I had to do it for Jesus or someone I specifically mentioned in my prayers. Otherwise, I was totally immobilized. It was just too painful!

I know that Jesus could only have suffered His passion for us; otherwise, it would not have been possible. He clearly showed me that this was true. On my way I had discovered three old spikes scattered amongst the rocks. This was truly our crucifixion that day. Miraculously, there were no ill affects afterwards, only some bloody knees which healed painlessly. Love conquers all!

As I headed for the Mountain of the Apparitions at 3:00 one morning in Medjugorje, I somehow missed the well-traveled path and ended up in an area totally alien to me. Flashes of lightening lit up the sky while thunder roared through the valley and surrounding hills. I eventually huddled in a small rocky grotto, perfumed by mountain herbs, where I prayed fervently amongst other things for the threatening storm to pass me by. Dogs barked in the valley below, but otherwise, silence reigned as the storm finally disappeared in the distance.

Since there were no recognizable landmarks present which could show me how to find my way back down the mountain after the sun rose, I had to wait until some-one ascended the trail in the distance. What seemed like hours later, a few pilgrims appeared at least one-fourth of a mile away, and I was able to find my way across "no man's land" to familiar territory. Thank You, Lord! There was a lot of praying going on that night for everyone. That is for sure!

"Have Car, Will Travel"

When my husband retired from the Air Force and we left Washington, D.C., for Connecticut, I was convinced that I would never return to Maryland to visit my relatives by myself. It seemed too far away for me to visualize being able to manage such a trip in the car alone. However, this changed when first my mom became very ill and then my sister-in-law was bedridden for months before she died. As a result, I had to drive frequently between Annapolis and Connecticut by myself.

In the meantime, we purchased a cottage and an old farmhouse in New Hampshire, both of which required extensive renovation. Driving up and down the highway on weekends in order to work on these places became old hat. Time passed quickly as if we were only going a few miles from home. The scenery was so beautiful that the trips could be very enjoyable. Even though I was raised in Annapolis, Maryland, I felt as if I were going home every time we approached the mountains of New Hampshire.

After my husband's retirement, we moved from Connecticut to Virginia. Since we still had three children living in Connecticut, our driving time had now doubled. Eventually, I drove by myself from Virginia to Oklahoma, and then Virginia to Phoenix. Then, Scottsdale, Arizona, was our place of residence for almost three years. From there I frequently drove back and forth to the East Coast. When we moved to Idaho it was necessary to drive between there and Arizona.

This all took place when I was in my late fifties and early sixties. No way could I have managed such endeavors without the help of the angels.

When we were in the process of moving from Virginia to Arizona, my husband called me in Oklahoma one evening at 5:30 requesting that I leave right away in order to be in Scottsdale, Arizona, by the next day. Since I had just arrived the evening before and had an extremely busy day, I was not overjoyed by the thought of having to drive to Amarillo, Texas, that evening. As a result, as I drove into the brilliant light of the setting sun, a migraine headache developed which severely affected my vision. Should I turn around and head back to my daughter's house or should I continue on my journey? If God wanted me in Arizona the next day, He had to do something. He did! The headache vanished completely and I arrived in Amarillo around 11:00 that evening. After what seemed like only a few hours of sleep, I awakened and headed west. When I stopped at a gas station convenience store after two hours of driving, I expressed to the clerk my surprise at the absence of traffic on the road. He replied that it was only 5:00 in the morning. My watch said 7:00 a.m.! Somehow, I had forgotten to switch from East Coast time to Mountain Standard Time. Who needs sleep when the angels are helping to drive the car? I arrived in Phoenix around 4:00 that afternoon, amazingly refreshed.

The only way that I could possibly do all this driving by myself was to absolutely trust God with my welfare. He had to take care of me if I was doing His will and not mine. It could be a scary thought, but abandoning myself to His care, I knew the angels and the Blessed Mother were watching over me. Otherwise, there was no way I could have said "Yes" to such ventures. He always honors my trust. We must remember that nothing good is ever easy!

"Memorable Moments With God"

Retreats and conferences have always been special occasions for me to spend time with the Lord. Under these circumstances I have been able to strengthen my relationship with God and, therefore, have gotten to know myself in a deeper way.

My weekend at St. Augustine's on Staten Island was one of those memorable moments. The priest's homily, during Saturday Mass, was about St. Peter and what a klutz he was. As he elaborated on his subject by making statements about St. Peter's impulsive nature, I was able to relate completely to what he did. There were other statements about him falling over his own two feet that also resonated with me.

When it was time for the consecration, Father invited us to join him around the altar. In order to do this we had to climb numerous steps. As I stepped upward, I suddenly stumbled and fell head first into the arms of the celebrating priest! If he hadn't been there, I certainly would have landed on the floor. A friend of mine remarked that I was like St. Peter. She undoubtedly was speaking of St. Peter's klutzy nature and not his holiness. Let's face it, God can do anything with anyone, if He so desires, and we're willing to say, "Yes." Look at St. Peter!

On another conference weekend, I experienced freedom from a situation that had concerned me for months. At a healing Mass in February, the priest asked as he was praying over me if I could die for Jesus. I didn't know the answer. However, when I returned to my seat, I knew that it was "No." This revelation was not easy to deal with; since before this happened, I was convinced that I could do anything God desired of me. For several days afterwards I was tortured by my lack of faith and love, until life's other trials displaced these thoughts.

During a Saturday evening Mass several months later, I suddenly felt God was asking me once again if I could offer myself as a spiritual sacrifice united with Him on the altar. After much inner turmoil, I knew that I could say, "Yes." What an exaltation I felt at that moment! Today? Who knows? Hopefully, if the occasion ever arises where this is being asked of me, I will be able to lay down my life. Yes, Lord, I love You and others enough to do this.

While on a month's retreat in Nova Scotia, I was offered the opportunity to spend the night beside a lake in a tent by myself. Having never done this sort of thing before, I was not thrilled by the thought of being in the wilderness alone in the dark. It was not an easy decision to make, but I felt that it was a necessary part of my stay, and, as a result, an important step in my spiritual progress.

Likewise, when I felt called to spend Holy Thursday night on the mountain in Medjugorje by myself several years later, I could say, "Yes." One piece of the puzzle leads to another in our lives. You might call it building spiritual muscle. Just as you go to the gym to build physical muscle, you must do what you feel God is asking of you in order to build spiritual muscle. Neither of these endeavors are easy and can even be quite painful; especially if they are to be of any value physically or spiritually.

"Pathway to Heaven"

$\mathcal{A}$ lady I knew who had recently remarried, said to me that if she knew the first time what she now knew, there would not have been any reason for the divorce. The one who had to change was she. So many times I have encountered couples that were perfectly suited to one another but ended up divorcing over some strange incompatibility.

I find this to be particularly true for some couples during their forties. If the "top man" on the totem pole, (which more than likely has been the male for many years), is not willing to allow the woman to eventually rise and shine on her own instead of being a nobody in his shadow, then problems often develop. We must know who we are. We must have a sense of self; and, as a result, allow our partner to be him or herself. My husband once stated that after years of being well known in military circles and then becoming a corporate pilot, he became "Mr. Nancy Drummond." He was not exactly thrilled with his new identity.

In addition, competition can be most disastrous in our lives. I had two artist friends who were married for years, but competition in their forties presented an insurmountable problem for them. Their marriage was not able to survive. This was also true of another friend whose husband refused to accept her as a complete person. He wanted his wife to live up to his expectations as a corporate housewife. She was an extremely talented, eccentric lady who could not submerge her own individuality. She definitely outshone him in social situations. This was most difficult for him to handle, and their marriage ended on a very unhappy note.

God gave us all talents, and we are expected to use them. Do not envy the person who is given much, because much is then expected. Do not envy the individual who is different from you, because we are all unique. Concentrate on your own individuality and then give it to God! He will make you more yourself if you allow Him!

Women have tremendous power in their own right. They have a role as wife and mother, which is as influential and potent as anyone could possibly wish to be. Women who do not wish to get in touch with that deep spiritual inner-self, particular to women, are the ones who want to be in the male's ballpark. Often these women come from households where a mother has made an issue of male dominance and feels nothingness as a subservient human being. This sense of inadequacy is conveyed to the other females in the family. I agree with women's lib only to the extent that I believe women need to be paid equally.

Men are born of women, raised by women, and usually marry women. Most of them are not terribly fond of us (as sex symbols yes, but not as people). There is often a feeling of dependency, which they dislike intensely. I had to gain weight in my late thirties in order to be accepted as an individual with an intellect, and not someone to be dismissed as a mindless female. It took much perseverance on my part to achieve that status.

I find myself often unconsciously referring to weddings as funerals and funerals as weddings. My "Freudian slips" can be embarrassing at times, especially if I say that I'm going to a funeral when it is really a wedding. We better be willing to die to self in a marriage, or chances of success are very limited. Hopefully after death we will have a united relationship with God. I believe marriage is based on two people kicking each other up to heaven. It is a pretty strong statement, but a positive one. Someone once said to me that my husband and I were two rocks rubbing the edges off of each other. It's God's vehicle, which we have chosen, to help work our way to heaven. Hang in there! The process can be painful, but just don't give up! Remember too, it takes three for a successful marriage: you, your spouse, and God!

By the way, my husband said he has allowed me to be me because he has not been able to change me in fifty years!

"Look for Jesus in Everyone!"

On my first trip to Medjugorje, Father, who was our spiritual leader, asked me to accompany him to the home of one of the seers. While we walked down a dirt road towards the young man's house, we were suddenly confronted by a lady with her goats who had popped out of the bushes onto our path. Her appearance with jet-black hair, white skin, numerous bloody scratches from the bramble bushes, and ragged clothing, gave us quite a jolt to say the least! As we gazed at her frightful appearance, she vanished into the bushes, only to reappear again a short distance from us.

Upon our return from the visionary's house, we again were literally accosted by this peasant woman. I knew God was asking me to kiss her, just as St. Francis had been asked to kiss the leper. I did do this, but it was not easy. She kept approaching Father in such a manner that I felt she was asking him for alms. When I pointed this out to him, he explained to me that he only gave money to certain charities in the States. When he reluctantly approached her with alms, she vigorously shook her head. What she apparently wanted from Father was a blessing and not money. Not everyone is hooked to the material. Even those in great need can find God to be more of a treasure than gold!

There have been memorable moments for me when I have been called to give to beggars; and, as a result, have had Jesus come leaping out of them in gratitude. One such incident occurred when I was climbing the mountain in Medjugorje. I came upon a young man who was asking for alms, and I knew I had to respond. He then came forth with a message for me that could only have come from God. Only the Lord would have known what I needed to hear at that moment!

Likewise, a crippled girl in Mexico extended her hand to me in a most heavenly response to my alms giving. To give or not to give to beggars on the street can present quite a dilemma for all of us. Does this person desire money for bona fide bodily needs, or is he a drug user or alcoholic merely trying to feed his addiction? I feel we should give to whoever asks and allow God to be concerned about what they do with what they have received. Never have I given to anyone who did not respond, "God bless you!" Maybe I really needed God's blessing that day, no matter what the source. We can look for Jesus in everyone!

"The High and the Low"

Heights have always presented a problem for me. When I visited Masada in the Holy Land, a high hill where the Jews made their last stand against the Romans, I was very relaxed in the cable car while crossing the valley. However, when I had to climb the steps within the narrow iron railings, which went up the face of the mountain, I panicked! There were numerous steps to navigate from where the cable car landed to the top. For me, this was very frightening.

Going down the mountain did not seem difficult because I was sermonizing to some nice lady. As a result, I was totally out of touch with my fear. I was only in touch with my mouth! Likewise, a lady on an airplane was speaking to me about how afraid she was as the airplane prepared to land. There had been a terrifying experience in her past that still caused great apprehension during a plane's descent. We engaged in a very animated conversation while we approached the runway, and afterwards, when I asked if she had been very afraid, she replied, "Not at all." Just keep talking and praying, it works!

On a visit to La Salette Shrine in the French Pyrenees Mountains, I could not bring myself to follow a group of pilgrims who were navigating a narrow path along the side of the mountain. Without any division between outer space and me, my fear of heights would not allow me to do it. I guess there wasn't anyone for me to preach to at that moment, Lord!

While touring the catacombs in Rome, our pilgrimage group came to an abrupt halt at the exact moment that I happened to be alone in a small cave-like portion of the passage. I was unable to move for at least five minutes. I was extremely traumatized. Claustrophobia was not a constant problem for me, but on that particular day it took a lot of prayer to be able to handle the situation without becoming totally panic stricken. I have been in many caverns where it would have been possible to experience fear under similar circumstances, but I was not susceptible at that moment. Thank You, Lord!

During my pregnancy with my fifth child, Chris, I was driving home one night to Delaware from Annapolis when the intermittent flashing of light and shadow from the superstructure of the Chesapeake Bay Bridge made me extremely nauseous. For several years after this experience I had serious problems with a similar sensation while driving through tunnels. Eventually, after much prayer, I recovered from the dread of entering such a passageway. Thankfully, today it is only a vague memory!

"Gethsemane in Medjugorje"

In 1991, I found myself climbing in Medjugorje. I was determined to spend from 7:00 p.m. Holy Thursday evening until 7:00 a.m. Good Friday morning on the Holy Hill. I was quite certain that this was what God was requesting me to do; however, just to be sure, I asked a priest in my pilgrimage group for his discernment. His response to me was, "It's just fine for you, but definitely not for me!"

I dressed very warmly in preparation for a cool evening on the mountain. My only extra possessions were my woolen cape, a rosary, and my flashlight. Around 11:00 that night I spread out my cape on the ground and attempted to relax while I prayed fervently for peace, because in the shadows nearby was a lone male who kept circling the area around me. After feeling greatly threatened by his actions, I decided to position myself closer to the cross near the apparition site. I used the large rocks in the area as a backrest, which gave me a more secure feeling. It seemed to be the wise thing to do.

Once again the hill appeared to be deserted; however, out of the dark materialized two men chatting animatedly with each other. They were extremely startled when I spoke up from out of the shadows asking them if they'd like to say a rosary. They reacted as though they were hearing a voice from beyond. While the three of us prayed the Sorrowful Mysteries, I experienced the most bone-chilling cold that I had ever encountered in my entire life along with a sense of incredible aloneness both of which Jesus must have suffered in the Garden the night of his passion.

When these gentlemen departed, three German youths arrived with a guitar and very quietly sang for several hours. In the distance were a small group of adults chanting near another cross, which penetrated the stillness of the night.

By 3:00 a.m. everyone had vanished and there was complete silence, except for the sounds of the dogs barking in the valley. A full moon had risen over the mountain, and there was much time to contemplate the Lord's passion before daybreak. For me it was a never-to-be forgotten Holy Thursday/Good Friday experience.

"Songs to Remember"

At a meeting for First Holy Communion parents, Sister played a song which I had never heard before but found to be most impressive. When someone asked her what the title was she announced, "Hosea."

Likewise, I decided to purchase a tape of the Western Priory Monks at the local religious bookstore. When I played the music at home, much to my surprise, "Hosea" was one of the recordings. What a great gift this was, and my family listened to "Hosea" night and day for an entire month. Once I hooked into a song at that time in my life, the saturation point was slow to come!

Another encounter was when we arrived Friday evening at St. Augustine's on Staten Island for our conference weekend. When my prayer group ladies and I proceeded to the chapel for the opening Mass, "Hosea" was the entrance song that night. I knew then and there that it was going to be an exceptional weekend with God. "Fear did not keep us apart!" are words from the song. Jesus had actually come to me the evening before, but this was the exclamation point! My honeymoon with God was an incredible experience that weekend!

"On Eagle's Wings" was another song which also spoke to me the first time I heard it. While in Medjugorje one cloudy, drizzly evening in October, we encountered several people coming off the mountain. One of the gentleman mentioned that he had sung "On Eagle's Wings" at the University of Notre Dame charismatic conference in the spring and offered to give us a repeat performance. It was truly a memorable moment for all of us as the strong male voice resounded throughout the darkened, silent valley.

When I was awakened from a deep sleep at 2:00 one morning, I became aware of the possibility of an evil presence manifesting itself near my bed. My husband was on a trip but my two young children were at home sound asleep. The only thing I could think to do at the time was sing "Be Not Afraid" loudly in order to alleviate the fear which was gripping me at that instant. I was grateful that my singing did not awaken my kids. Listening to their mom singing at the top of her lungs at such a time of the night would have been quite disturbing! It worked, however, and peace soon returned!

"Is Listening Important?"

My daughter Carol and I were flying to Medjugorje with Swissair Airlines. As a result of a five-hour layover in Zurich early that morning, our pilgrimage group decided to spend this cold, drizzly day sightseeing. We were not particularly interested in window-shopping, so we decided to separate ourselves from our fellow travelers. Somehow we ended up in a park area and decided to explore a wooded path near the river. We were trying to kill time until a museum nearby opened. Carol spied an unusual looking waterfowl along the shore and vanished from sight in order to get a snapshot of this large bird. Soon afterwards, I became aware of a pair of trousers, which kept disappearing into the bushes each time I glanced over my left shoulder. At first I was not sure that I was seeing correctly, but then realized the "pants" were coming closer! Undoubtedly, someone was trying to sneak up on me, but was not able to do so since I kept turning around, causing him to plunge back into the vegetation along the path. His pant legs gave him away. Miraculously, my daughter was listening that morning because when I called for her to come she responded almost immediately. We hurried past the bushes where my swarthy stalker was visible. Thankfully, we departed from the area in one piece, unscathed! Thank You, Lord!

While on a pilgrimage to La Salette Shrine in the French Pyrenees Mountains, I was standing in a Swiss airport talking with some of my fellow travelers. All of a sudden I became aware of a young girl who dashed away from our vicinity and disappeared into the crowd. My immediate reaction was to ask myself, could she have taken my wallet? Unfortunately, this is exactly what had happened. Obviously, the closure on my pocketbook was not secure enough to prevent a pickpocket easy access to my wallet.

Before I left on this trip, my husband had informed me that it was not wise to carry the purse which I had planned to take. He even went so far as to buy me another bag; however, I chose to reject it because of its ungainly size. Oh, Lord, I was not listening! The good news was that I had previously removed all my credit cards, license, and money, except for thirty dollars. The bad news was that I had left some credit card slips in the wallet, which made my card number accessible to the thief.

This situation presented a dilemma. Was I supposed to phone my husband and inform him of what had taken place, or did I only need to turn it over to God and trust that all would be well? This was the beginning of our pilgrimage; therefore, such an incident could have been a real deterrent to having a peaceful week with God. After much prayer, I felt God was saying it would be all right. There was no need to upset my husband with a phone call. I needed to trust God; so, every time I thought of the possibility of someone using those credit slips, I turned it over to the Lord. It turned out to be a very spirit-filled pilgrimage!

Eventually, when I talked to the credit card people upon my return to the States, they felt that since no action had been taken by then, it was highly unlikely that there would ever be a problem. Thank You, Lord. There never was. I was listening...at least part of the time!

"Two to Tango"

I was always pretty much of a lone-ranger when it came to evangelizing, and so was my friend, Elaine. God, however, showed me very clearly during our stay in Idaho why He sent out His disciples two-by-two. For one thing, neither of us was able to hook into everyone in our presence. Half of the folks found me someone they could relate to and the other half, my friend Elaine. It definitely took the two of us to cover most bases. What one would leave out, the other was able to supply.

We are very different people, but much alike in some respects, both of us being pushy broads! If either of us had been more reticent than the other it would have never worked. One of us would have been completely destroyed by the other. In Idaho, we spent many hours driving in a car. Each of us can be very questionable with our driving skills at times. A sense of humor was an absolute necessity because there were tense moments when we definitely felt the need to eliminate the other fellow. God is good! He managed to have us both survive with our friendship still intact. Fortunately, we have a deep respect for one another. The bottom line is, we recognized the need for one another and we are still two to tango with God!

When presenting your viewpoint to others, it is most important to simply state what you believe. To say that I am right and that you are wrong is an excellent way to turn the other fellow off. The best approach is to say to yourself, "Come into my parlor, said the spider to the fly." However, when evangelizers appear on your doorstep, you better be very knowledgeable about your own beliefs before you issue an invitation. Many times I have felt that they are not sure who is evangelizing whom and often ask if they may return.

After Mass, Elaine and I were driving with Father one evening on treacherous mountain roads. It was a ter-rifying experience for me to be seated next to him in the front seat. As he barreled along the icy highway, I com-mented, "Father, I'm not ready to die tonight!" He was silent for a short period of time before he exclaimed, "You ladies have nothing to worry about; since God doesn't want you up there telling Him what He is doing wrong!" Maybe it is okay to tell God what you think He is doing wrong. Just don't tell the folks you are trying to evangel-ize to what they are doing wrong!

My meeting of spiritual people all over the world has been very much a revelation to me. In spite of differ-ent religious beliefs, when I encounter someone with a deep sense of God, I am very aware of a bond that exists between us.

God made everyone in His image and likeness, not just a special few. He is in everyone, and we must be aware of that fact. God never made trash! Some of us have tried to get to know, love, and serve Him, and others have not. If the God within us has been activated, He touches others without. Being and not speaking may very often be the answer. A smile or a simple touch may be all that is required. It is what you are and not necessarily what you say, unless the Holy Spirit is using you as His mouthpiece. If that is true, then you are definitely making an impression with whomever you are called to speak.

Father MacNamara once said that there are two ways to take God's name in vain; by cursing and by talking about a God you have not experienced. You better know Him before you open your mouth!

"Brooms are for Sweeping"

My friend Andy said to me that dreams about others are more than likely about us. I had just related a very thought-provoking dream to her which I had concerning a friend of mine who was a monk. I visualized an iron cot in his room with much garbage tossed underneath. Crumpled balls of paper were piled high at either end of the bed, and in the middle was a bright red piece of trash. My remark to her was, "He certainly has a lot of garbage under his bed!" She exclaimed, "It's yours, not his!"

At a healing Mass shortly afterwards, when Father asked me if I could die for Jesus, I realized this was the red piece of garbage under the bed which I had to handle. Could I or couldn't I? At the time I thought not, but months later at another Mass during the consecration, I again felt confronted with the same question. At least for the moment I felt that I could. Hopefully, if the occasion ever presented itself whereby I was put to the test, I could give my life for the Lord or a friend.

A year later, I attended a Mass one Saturday evening which was the last Advent service before Christmas. As I left my house for church, I grabbed a small Asian broom to bring to Brother as a present. Interestingly enough, someone in the past had informed me that brooms were the sign of a monk. While the service was in progress it occurred to me that I had to give Brother the broom and tell him to sweep out the garbage from under his bed. This had to take place before Christmas, which was less than a week off. I knew that he was not going to be cheerfully receptive to what I had to say. He exclaimed to me, "I don't have any garbage under my bed!" Out of my mouth came, "Whether you have any garbage under your bed or not does not concern me. But if you do, you'd better get rid of it before Christmas."

On Christmas Eve at midnight I was back at the church waiting for Mass to begin when a lady appeared at my side telling me she had Christmas presents in her shopping bag for both the Father and Brother who were in residence. It was a cold, snowy wintry night, so she expressed a desire for me to walk with her to her car after the service. Naturally, I agreed to do this, and she seemed relieved.

When Mass was over, we went to look for the recipients of her presents but could only locate Father who said Brother must have gone to his hermitage. The lady asked if I would go with her to Brother's pad in order that she might personally deliver his gift to him. While I waited outside, standing on a huge rock under a full moon, she reappeared at his door and then disappeared within for at least five minutes. Because I stood in the extreme cold wearing a light leather coat, I was not all that pleased. Finally, they appeared in the doorway. Brother dashed over to where I was standing and whispered in my ear, "I did a lot of sweeping with that broom!"

He subsequently left the area shortly thereafter! When I first met Brother, I made the statement to Andy that he wasn't supposed to be residing where he was at the time. She told me, "You're probably going to worry him right out of there!" God sent a crazy lady with seven kids to be a thorn in his flesh! He did not like it one bit! Could it be the simple confounding the wise?

"Sport for Thought"

As I arrived on the lacrosse field after the high school game was well underway, I happened to overhear the lady standing next to me yelling for her son to kill the person who was playing the same position on the opposing team. "Hit him! Hit him with your stick!" she screamed. The player whom she was prodding her son to hit with his stick just happened to be my son! I moved quickly away before I felt compelled to say something uncharitable to her.

When my sons, Chris and Dick, who both played lacrosse for years, sustained an injury, it took forever for it to heal. Their opponents were constantly hitting them in the exact same area. Any bandage, obvious wound, or bruise would be an open invitation to the opposing team.

The lacrosse coach of their team had an outstanding record. One day I felt called to tell him how much I disliked the game. If I had taken a gun and shot him, his reaction could not have been more pronounced. He was devastated by my remark. Remember, Indians used this game when they did not wish to actually wage war to settle disputes. Lacrosse was the next best thing.

Have you ever observed referees who are so intent upon having one team win rather than the other that their judgment is severely affected and they are extremely unfair in their decision-making? Under these circumstances, parents can go absolutely wild. Who needs this sorry aggravation in their life?

When my granddaughter Lisa lived with us for a year in Idaho, I had great difficulty going to her basketball games and rooting for their team to win. It occurred to me that in cheering for the home team I was in reality expressing my desire for the other side to lose. Suddenly this seemed very wrong! I could not visualize Jesus wanting one side to win and the other side to lose.

Sports are great exercise, but when carried to the extreme, which we have managed to do, there is something drastically wrong with our mentality. Today, young people with their sports heroes have mostly abandoned the desire to imitate individuals who are worthy of their adulation.

The Blessed Mother told a seer whom I know that karate was a sophisticated form of violence. If this is true, than so is boxing, wrestling, and other serious contact sports. They were certainly events which the pagan world participated in during the time of Christ. While watching a professional football game, it occurred to me that this was nothing more than a pseudo-war in which the players were engaged. Since I was always an extremely competitive individual, to simply play a game for enjoyment and not become upset over the consequences was difficult for me. While playing paddle tennis in the 60s, I knew it was time to let go of my great desire to win and just sit back and allow God, through me, to hit that ball. He does a great job! I was free and relieved of all the pressure I used to apply to myself.

"Stop and Listen!"

My husband Speight and I had just left Gonzales, Louisiana. We were on our way home to Virginia when I expressed the desire to stop at McDonald's for my usual morning orange juice pick-me-up. Speight felt that we should get out of the New Orleans traffic rush as soon as possible. He, therefore, suggested that I wait until later to satisfy my yearning. As we headed south on I-10, dense fog covered the road making visibility nil. It was almost impossible to read the huge green signs which covered the highway. Once we headed into Mississippi the traffic subsided and we were able to breathe a sigh of relief. Only minutes later came an announcement over the radio that there had been an eighty car pileup in an area through which we had passed maybe five minutes prior! It was such a disaster that it took eight hours to clear away the debris. Thank God I listened to my husband that morning. If we had stopped to get my orange juice, who knows what would have happened to us?

❖　❖　❖

One day Speight greeted me at the airport when I had returned from a visit to Oklahoma. He surprised me with a new truck that he had purchased in my absence. I was not overly impressed with his choice initially. However, the vehicle was adequate and I gradually grew attached to it. The red cab with the gray camper top was attractive, but he informed me that a red top to match the cab was on order. Since I liked the color combination we had, I asked him to tell the dealer that we would prefer to keep the gray one.

Subsequently, one morning while in Arizona, my husband went to get into the truck which had been parked in the driveway. To his surprise, there sat the vehicle minus the cab! What occurred to me later was, if I had accepted the red top it probably would still have been there. A gray top could fit in anywhere, but a bright red one? That was highly unlikely. I was not listening back then. What I learned is that doing it my way is not always the right way!

When I was driving from Taos, New Mexico, to Colorado, the wonderful scenery enraptured me. As a result, I did not have the slightest inclination to exceed the 55mph speed limit. Outside of a small town near the Colorado border, I accelerated in order to pass a large truck which had pulled out in front of me. Unfortunately, it was then that I heard the police siren! He was absolutely right, I was speeding, even if only momentarily!

Because I received the ticket just prior to going to a retreat center in Colorado for the following month, I needed to take care of the ticket immediately. As a result, when I entered the post office parking lot it occurred to me that I needed to finish several personal letters that should have also been completed before the retreat. The letter writing was definitely unfinished business that God was giving me a second chance to accomplish. I resisted doing them for weeks. God is tough and He certainly got my attention, as well as my money that day! A police siren will do it every time!

My family was busy completing renovations on our old farmhouse in New Hampshire. One Sunday during this time I drove through a neighboring village and noticed an interesting garage sale in progress. I had discovered some old windows that we definitely could use, as well as an antique copper heater that was aesthetically pleasing. Buying stuff on Sundays has always been a no-no in my book; however, back then I could not resist the temptation. After I brought home my treasures, my husband requested that I proceed to the hardware store to pick up something he badly needed at the moment. As I started to back out of my driveway, I heard a horrible crunching sound. It turned out to be the total destruction of the wonderful copper heater. I ran over it! This incident happened after I knew God was telling me that I should not put old junk in the house anymore. It was a message that clearly told me no more collectibles, only necessities. He certainly eliminated that old useless object immediately, and allowed me to do it all by myself. Easy come; easy go, particularly when we are not listening!

"Colorful God"

My daughter Carol, a teacher in a Catholic school in Louisiana, traveled to Medjugorje with me during the Thanksgiving break. In her possession were numerous rosaries which she had collected from various students. They were to be presented when the Blessed Mother made her scheduled appearance to the children of the St. James Church during the evening Mass. When she opened the tightly wrapped bundle after Mary's visitation, she was greeted by a multitude of shining gold rosary beads! The one that impressed her most was a rosary in many pieces, which she had persuaded a very troubled youth in one of her classes to relinquish. Because of its poor condition he did not feel that it was worthy to be presented to Our Lady for her blessing. The Blessed Mother was clearly showing him that she loved us all, particularly in our brokenness!

On one of my trips to Medjugorje I met a gentleman who had come to Yugoslavia not totally convinced that the Blessed Mother was appearing as he had heard. One afternoon he came running up to me bursting with excitement. As he stood that morning on the big mountain, he had watched a lady's beads turn to gold as she said the rosary. He was overwhelmed by his experience. God is most impressive, particularly when we open our hearts to believing that "nothing is impossible with Him!"

A friend of mine told me that her rosary turned to gold one Saturday morning at 9 a.m. as she stood in line for confession. This was a very devout lady, full of love for the Blessed Mother and the Lord. It is not for us to decide when or where!

I had purchased numerous dollar "angel" rosary beads at the Fatima Shrine in Portugal and decided to present one of these to my sister-in-law, who is not a Catholic. She welcomed the gift. Many months later when I asked her about it, she brought forth from her pocketbook a gleaming gold rosary. This was most assuredly God's gift to a very "special" holy lady!

"A Christmas to Remember"

My Christmas gift from God one year was an unforgettable experience that took place at Midnight Mass in Connecticut.

There was an obviously intoxicated lady sitting in the pew directly in front of me with a six-month old baby boy. The child was dressed in a short-sleeved black velvet suit and brief pants that left his small white limbs totally exposed. Since it was a bitterly cold night, I felt great sympathy for this child who must have been cold. As the Mass progressed I was able to imagine this baby as the Christ child, visualizing the wounds in his little hands and feet. With such a mother, it was very possible he was going to suffer much during his lifetime. I wept profusely throughout the entire Mass. I experienced a Jesus whose mother, knowing full well the prophecies for the Messiah, had to have encountered great sorrow in the midst of incredible joy. How could I not remember this Christmas morning forever?

"Don't Ignore It"

After my husband had his auto accident, my daughter Carol came from Louisiana for a short visit while her dad was still in the hospital. That Friday evening we decided to attend Amazing Grace's healing service. While there, Carol seemed certain that she recognized a young male in the audience that was an old acquaintance of hers. As it turned out, he was not the person she thought he was; however, God placed the desire in her heart to try to get in touch with this individual while she was on the East Coast. She felt that she needed to ask his forgiveness for any heartache she might have caused him in the past. She was successful in finding this person and felt great healing in the process.

One past August was a busy time in our lives. The first part of the month I spent in Louisiana, and the second part in Connecticut and the San Juan Islands off the coast of Washington. When we returned to Connecticut from the West Coast, we drove to New Hampshire, where I knew we had to look for a house near the La Salette Shrine in Enfield. My husband had some reservations about this decision, but decided to go along rather amicably with what I felt God was asking us to do.

Amazingly, there was only one house available which was located directly across from the Shrine. Nothing but a grassy meadow separated us from this holy place. In fact, you could look almost directly from my bedroom window into the chapel window which was near the Tabernacle. This was the Lord's gift to us, most assuredly!

It was not an inexpensive piece of property. Although God had given us gifts in the past that were great bargains, this was not possible in recent years. Doing what I feel He is asking of me does not come cheap! In actuality, it is His money; therefore, I guess He wants us to spend it on His desires regardless if they are not our own.

When we returned to our home in Virginia from our visit to New Hampshire, our friends, who had been using our house during a hurricane, (they had lost their electricity) mentioned that there had been an interesting message on the answering machine. A real estate agent had called asking us if we'd like to sell our home. Since she had sold a house only a few doors away, she still had some clients interested in the area. However, we decided to attempt to sell our property without involving a realtor. On Thursday we placed in the yard a "For Sale" sign, which had been left in the basement by a previous owner, and by Sunday a buyer appeared and bought it for cash!

I believed God was saying, "Sell it and move to New Hampshire now!" Never have I felt that I ever received a more immediate request from Him. The real estate agent in New Hampshire had called asking us if we would consider renting the house to an interested party until June; however the answer had to be "No." Actually, to have two seventy-year-olds move to such a cold climate at the end of October did not make a lot of sense. Nevertheless, my discernment was not to move in June, but in October!

We moved as planned and certainly found how important it was for us to be there. Since we had three children who lived in Connecticut, we were able to visit back and forth many times. We had decided that when we moved this far north we would spend the winters in a warmer part of the country; therefore, Arizona was our home for three months, and I was able to work on my writings during that time. In addition, our son Dick and his family spent numerous weekends in our house during our absence. This was a difficult time in his life so he needed to get away. Since that time they have also built a house in the same development and now live there permanently!

God said the house in New Hampshire was purchased to save lives. Are we not supposed to lay down our lives for one another?

"Don't Take Yourself Too Seriously"

I received a phone call one morning asking if Nancy was there. To this inquiry I replied, "No, she isn't." The woman on the other end of the line then proceeded to tell me that Nancy had left her MasterCard in their store that morning while shopping. I then exclaimed, "That's me!" There was a long silence on the other end of the line. For you see, my daughter Nancy was home from college and had left to visit a friend in the neighborhood. Since I did not recognize the lady's voice, I just assumed she wished to speak to my daughter and not to me. When I explained this to the caller, I'm not so sure she believed me. I think she was convinced that she was speaking to a total nut – a real fruitcake!

My daughter Mary Lou was getting married in August and had requested that I have the wedding invitations printed as soon as possible. When I went to place the order I was naturally asked where and when the wedding would take place. In addition, I was asked for the groom's name. Guess what? I did not know how to spell my future son-in-law's Polish last name. I informed him that I needed to go home, find out, and then call him back with the information. He seemed rather amazed with this fact and replied, "You don't know, lady?" How uninformed can a future mother-in-law be?

When my sister-in-law was in nursing school she had a three-month training session in the psychiatric ward of the hospital. There was a particular patient that she had found to be most interesting, for she would walk the halls singing repeatedly:

> I'm a little nut brown
> Laying on the cold, cold, ground
> Someone came and stepped on me
> That is why I'm cracked you see
> I'm a nut! I'm a nut! I'm a nut!

Hopefully when I lose it completely, I will remember this ditty!

As a teenager I was walking on the beach in Florida one day when I suddenly became aware that the top of my two-piece bathing suit had departed and was down around my waist. Since I was talking with a male friend at the time, I wrapped my arms around my chest and as dispassionately as possible asked, "Could you please rescue my top for me? It just slipped off my bosom." He hesitated for a few moments but then helped me to recover my top, as well as my dignity that day.

Many years ago, I was walking up the church aisle towards the altar at my confirmation Mass when lo and behold my garter belt suddenly snapped. I waddled forward toward the Bishop with my stockings down around my knees! I must have been establishing a very down-to-earth relationship with God at that moment. Likewise, my daughter Carol reminded me that the same thing happened to me at her wedding as I approached the priest for communion. The name of the game is to grin and bare it! God does need a few laughs from time to time.

Early one Saturday morning, three seven-year-olds headed for the U.S. Naval Academy in Annapolis for a morning of roller-skating. The walks there were great for that purpose since they sloped gently in several areas. However, after several hours of fun, we decided to enter a large gym where an exercise class was in session. Undetected, we headed for the balcony. While we observed the class in silence, all of a sudden my skate key slipped out of my hand and sped down the polished balcony and landed right in front of the instructor with a loud bang! Silence reigned and we fled. As we just reached the door, the very angry instructor stood in front of us and handed me my skate key and reminded us never to return again.

Ironically, many years later I returned to a similar balcony at the Academy with my midshipman friend for a basketball game. As my date and I cheered for the home team, my pocketbook suddenly left my lap. It plunged into space and landed on the Admiral's head and shoulder below us. I screamed out but to no avail, since everyone was screaming at that moment for the game. My poor underclass friend had to approach the Commandant of the

Naval Academy for his date's pocketbook. It took him a while to build up enough courage to do this, although fortunately the Admiral, from what I could tell, did not get hurt. This is certainly one way to make an impression on an Admiral and on your date. To be honest, I don't think he ever asked me out again. I was just too impressive!

A lady in our prayer group became very angry with me because she said that I was responsible for her second pregnancy. She was not young when she married, but had been gifted with one beautiful baby boy. Before our meeting began one morning, I laughingly told several of the young women present that I was going to pray for them to get pregnant. Having had seven children myself, I remarked it would be great for them to have more kids. When this gal did not appear in our group for several months, I was told she was now pregnant and held me personally responsible! At this time in her life she apparently believed one was enough. Never again did she come to our prayer meeting, but subsequently did give birth to a wonderful baby girl. Obviously our thoughts are not always God's thoughts—hardly ever, that is!

"Don't Judge"

I was never a good housekeeper in my youth. To be honest, I was pretty awful. Decorating was my passion, certainly not cleaning. With a house full of kids this meant messy surroundings much of the time, particularly a disorderly kitchen or bathroom. I always said that good housekeepers in the neighborhood would never have looked so great if I had not been around to provide the contrast. As I have gotten older, messy houses bother me tremendously. I'm much more apt to have a tidy home now than in the past. It's very difficult to find peace in the midst of disorder!

God has allowed me to make up for all the messiness in my past life by helping others who are bogged down with a house which they are unable to clean or organize. They either must move and can't figure out what to get rid of, or have the need to eliminate an excessive amount of belongings in their life, period. Sometimes it has been an illness in the family and the time to clean simply does not exist. Surprisingly, they have allowed me to help bring order into their chaos. In my messy days pride would not have permitted me to say, "Yes, I need your help!" I was always going to do it "tomorrow." It took years before I could accept myself and appreciate help from others. God loved me wherever I was at the moment, and I didn't have to clean up my act before I approached Him!

I've been a sugar addict all my life, but never really got into a full-blown addiction until after having my seventh child. With two babies and five teenagers in the house during the late 60s, I suppose sugar was the lesser of evils. God help the world if it had been drugs, alcohol, or sex. The old adage, "It takes one to know one" is absolutely true. God did send certain individuals into my life to reveal myself to me. One such person was a very manipulative friend who had at least five game plans lined up to evoke a certain response. If she perceived one game wasn't working well she would scrap that and move immediately to plan B, and so forth on down the line. If none of these were achieving the desired results, then intimidation was the last resort. People who are like us can be extremely irritating factors in our lives, particularly if we have not come to terms with our own humanity. This lady was a caricature of most of us and badly frightened a lot of people because she made an excellent mirror of their humanity. When I asked God about my controlling, manipulative self, I realized that I did not have the patience for all those game plans. I just said, "Do it!" However, I was able, at times, to see myself setting the stage for the response which I wished to evoke from someone. All of us have a game plan to a lesser or greater degree.

Today, I know that I perform in a very strange manner at times. It's interesting to watch those who are observing and disapproving of whatever they see. I can be guilty of being judgmental of others myself, but God is trying to show me that most people have a reason for their actions, of which we are not usually aware. Of course, many times I do things or say things and certainly wonder why. Don't judge folks! You do not know where the person is coming from or what their baggage may be! Remember, judge and be judged!

Truck drivers who would come barreling past me on the highway used to be an endless irritation to me. This was until I became the owner of a small automatic truck and moved out West from the East Coast. My attempts to navigate mountainous roads or steep hills became a real challenge. The vehicle did not have enough power to perform the way I thought it should on roads that were not flat. It made me understand why a truck driver did everything in his power not to have to shift gears in his ascent, even if it often made me feel as though I was encountering a monster on a roll. You cannot slow down once you've gathered momentum or you've lost it. Also, I was told that the incredible weight in the trailer is deadly if you must decelerate suddenly on the decline.

"Pilgrimage Potpourri"

My daughter Carol called me on the phone to say she really felt that her entire family, six kids and a husband, were supposed to go to Medjugorje. As of yet, God had not provided the funds to support such an undertaking. Tomorrow was the deadline to register for the pilgrimage; therefore, she had to come up with the money immediately. That evening I phoned her saying she should try the bank for a loan. Likewise, very early the next morning a lady friend called telling her she had a dream that clearly indicated Carol should go to the bank for the funds she needed. When she approached the officer at the bank he offered to lend her $6,000 against her car. This was a big surprise because she drove an old van. As a result, she and her family were able to get to Yugoslavia. Since her youngest child was only fifteen months old at the time, the trip was not easy—a great sacrifice. As a result, for her trust in the Lord she was given the gift of receiving messages from Jesus and the Blessed Mother. This has been a great grace for those who have been the recipients of God's bounty. God does provide, but never in the way we expect. Pennies did fall from heaven, but not out of the sky, only by way of the bank for Carol and her family.

When I first started traveling on pilgrimages and participating in retreats, I decided a camera was an absolute necessity. For instance, the day before I was to leave for my Nova Scotia retreat, I bought a small compact camera for the trip; however, the next morning it would not work! Obviously, God was trying to tell me not to bring a camera! If I had brought a camera with me on my numerous travels, I would never have been there for God—more for people, places, and things. Since He knows me very well, undoubtedly, it is not what He had in mind!

Every pilgrimage for me has incorporated the Joyful, the Sorrowful, and the Glorious Mysteries. When life is extremely difficult the week before I am to leave on a trip, I know it's going to be a wonderfully rewarding and spiritual experience. Even though going through the Sorrowful mysteries can be a most painful encounter, in order to get to the Glorious ones, I must go through the passion. The catch is not to allow this trying period to negatively affect my entire pilgrimage. I must not dwell on my pain once it has passed. The ecstasy cannot be had without the agony; there is no other way! Remember to offer up your suffering for love of Jesus and for saving souls. This can turn a difficult experience into a joyful one!

On pilgrimages, women who are similar to me inevitably do not like me. Pushy broads are not often comfortable around other pushy broads unless they have developed a sense of humor about themselves. I'm also a vegetarian, and cooks in foreign countries seem to dislike any American who does not eat meat. They see this as much more of a problem than it really is, since a piece of cheese or a boiled egg will do. This problem presented itself on a flight to China. The steward was so angry with me for being a vegetarian that he told me he hoped they would keep me there. I told him if they kept me, more than likely they would keep him too since we were together!

People often ask me why my husband does not accompany me on my pilgrimages. The answer to that question is that he would be perfectly miserable. As a pilot in the Air Force and later a corporate pilot, he was responsible for running a smooth operation. Being on time was the name of the game. On a pilgrimage, one has to hang loose. People are always late and seemingly, schedules are for breaking, not for keeping. At least that is the way it often appears. My husband would find all of this extremely difficult to handle. To have a successful pilgrimage you cannot allow anything to upset you. There again, there is no ecstasy without the agony!

On a pilgrimage where you are trying to listen and do God's will, you are not likely to win any popularity contests with your fellow travelers. God could not care less if you're pleasing anyone else except Him! For example, on one of my trips, we were in the Philippines during a typhoon. I had not heard our director mention it to us on the plane the previous day. After I prayed with my roommate early the next morning, we both believed,since I was not feeling well that I should stay in bed most of the day. Why the wind was blowing at gale forces outside my window was a complete mystery to me. All I knew was that I needed to stay put and pray for everyone. Suddenly, one of the hotel windows blew out, and when a workman appeared to fix it, he informed me that we were in the midst of a typhoon. We would have had an incredible amount of water in our room that night if someone had not been present to get in touch with hotel maintenance immediately. From the reaction of those who braved the storm, I was definitely considered a "chicken" for not having accompanied them to the sched-uled holy spot that day. By the way, I am a really "big chicken," except when God is saying, "Do it." I would rather die doing it than not doing it, most of the time!

In China, there again, I did not feel called to go with the group to the Great Wall. I had been in China once before and did not think a repeat visit was what God wanted from me that day. Thankfully, when several ladies returned to the hotel by themselves early in the evening with a lady doctor who was having an obvious appendicitis attack, I was there to give them assistance. However, when they requested that I go to the hospital with them, I felt God wanted me to stay at the hotel. They were obviously not happy with my decision, but it defi-nitely was the right one. As it turned out, a lady who would never have assumed the role of spokesman for the group had no choice but to perform the duty. God knows what He's doing! We don't need to, but don't assume anyone else will understand either. Being the bad guy when you're trying to hook up with God is inevitable!

"God's Planned Encounter"

In traveling around the country, my husband and I have encountered many interesting people whom God used to speak to us in various ways. For instance, one particular week we were staying in a condo in North Carolina. There I was used to making an afternoon visit to the local church, which became a daily ritual for me. It was a peaceful time to spend with God. Likewise, golf is my husband's passion since his retirement, but it's definitely not mine. He maintains that God teaches him great humility on the golf course. My comment is, "If you're not incorporating this into your everyday life, then it's worthless." I only hope that God plays golf. Mother Angelica once said, "Just be careful you don't go down that black hole some day with the ball!"

At the church one afternoon was a gentleman taking pictures of the altar who told me he was writing a book about various church interiors. After the next morning Mass we bumped into each other again as we were leaving. My husband asked if he would like to join us for breakfast, an invitation he readily accepted. Immediately after our meal, my husband had a golf engagement. Prior to his leaving however, he extended an invitation to this man to spend the night if he would like to stay in the area another day. He accepted the offer and it was up to me to entertain the chap until Speight could join us once more.

This former art professor was now traveling around the country. We chatted most of the day about his former life, which had been full of a great deal of pain. We all have our baggage, that's for sure; and it's often easier to reveal ourselves to a stranger than to someone who knows us well. Since I needed to make numerous copies of a "forgiveness prayer" which I was taking to Norfolk, Virginia, the next day, he joined me in my endeavor. This powerful prayer touched him enough for him to express a desire to distribute it to various churches he planned to visit on his journey South, as well as to utilize it for his own personal use. A priest in Medjugorje initially gave it to me. For many years I have been called to distribute it, particularly during the Advent and Lenten seasons. Unloading our garbage to make room for God is most important in our lives.

That evening he brought an icon he had painted into the condo and the Holy Spirit blew me away. It was unbelievable how much power was emulating from his painting. I was told that much prayer, as well as nine coats of paint, went into the production of an icon. I had experienced the same sensation while visiting the Vatican Collection at the Metropolitan Museum many years ago. There were several artifacts displayed that gave off a similar sense of God's presence.

We were also afforded the opportunity to say the rosary together that evening. This turned out to be a very great gift. Our gentleman friend had his mother's rosary with him, but had not said this powerful prayer for twenty-three years. He expressed his gratitude for being given the opportunity to do this once more. How much we would have all missed if my husband had not extended an invitation for this gentleman to spend the night! Speight was definitely "listening" to God that morning!

"Hang Loose"

When my friend Elaine and I drove up the Merrit Parkway toward Bridgeport, Connecticut, I missed my turnoff. Because there was extensive road construction in the area, I was not able to immediately double back to the desired exit. Since our schedule had been interrupted for the afternoon, we were both extremely frustrated by my mistake. Still annoyed, we stopped to eat much later than we originally anticipated. In the midst of our lunch a woman whom I did not recognize approached our table. She apparently knew me and wished to share her story with us.

She proceeded to tell us that at a meeting three years ago where she and I had been present, I had made several statements concerning God with which she had vigorously disagreed. Suddenly, a few months ago, she understood clearly what had been said. I remembered that several members of the group had received my remarks with great hostility that morning.

If we had been on schedule, as planned, most likely we would not have encountered this lady. This was truly a gift from God.

But the journey did not stop there. On our way to the local high school, Elaine and I, in order to seek information about the possibility of her son's attendance there in the near future, took a back road which ended up not being the shortcut we anticipated. It was definitely the long way around since the street was badly torn up, plus it exited well past our destination. While Elaine was speaking to one of the school officials, a young man appeared who was able to give her information concerning various sports activities as well as his phone number so that her son would have the opportunity to speak personally to one of his peers. If we had arrived on the scene earlier, this student may not have been available. School was not in session at the time and he just happened to be there at the moment. Just remember nothing is accidental with God!

Early one morning we were in Southern California looking for the Benedictine Monastery. After making numerous wrong turns and receiving misleading information from the locals, we finally arrived at our destination at 11:00 a.m. Mass was just starting. If we had arrived earlier, most likely we would have departed before the service and missed a most joyful celebration with the monks.

God's timing is not always our timing. He has shown me numerous times not to get upset with circumstances beyond my control! It may turn out to be the "right" time after all!

"Escape Impossible"

I had just driven into my son's driveway after having dinner with a friend, when through the woods I could see a neighbor's house on fire. My son, with two of his friends, immediately dashed over to see if they could be of help. They found an unconscious male at the base of the staircase, which they hauled out into the yard. In the meantime, my daughter-in-law, a doctor in her residency, had just returned from her walk and was called upon to give life support to this bloody individual. Despite all her efforts he perished on the way to the hospital in the ambulance.

It wasn't until later in the evening that the rescue crew found four more bodies in the house. It was also discovered that they all had been shot. This tragedy occurred the evening before the Oklahoma bombing; therefore, it did not receive national publicity, as it normally would have. Apparently, the owner of the house was in conflict with his young tenants and decided to rid himself of them once and for all. He subsequently was convicted and sentenced for all five murders.

Just two months later, in June, I left my home one evening and headed for the local church in a neighboring town. It was in the northeastern corner of Idaho, a relatively rural area of the state. As I drove toward the main highway, I was stopped by a police officer about three miles from my house and asked if I had noticed anything unusual in the area. They were obviously searching for someone, but they did not give me any details at the time. When I returned around 10:00 p.m., I encountered a roadblock on the main highway and was told to go straight home. "Make sure your house is securely locked tonight," the Policeman said.

Early the next morning as we were driving up the hill, we observed numerous cars parked in the driveway of the house located two doors from ours. What had occurred, we were told, was that a policeman had stopped a car which was driving erratically on the main highway the previous evening. When he approached the driver to ask for his license, the young man pulled out a gun and shot him. Amazingly, the cop had on his bulletproof vest that day. Consequently, he was not injured; however, his assailant took off on an access road heading toward the river. He and his girlfriend then abandoned their vehicle and were hiding somewhere in the vicinity. The police surmised that they could possibly be following the waterway but at the time were not able to locate them.

By the next morning the culprits were discovered in the barn next door to us. The male refused to give himself up to the police and subsequently shot and killed himself; whereas, the girl chose to surrender. Apparently, the driver and his friend had been using drugs, had stolen the car on the East Coast, and had subsisted on stolen credit cards.

When we think we can remove ourselves from the violence which is going on in this country today by moving to a sparsely populated area of the States, we are sadly mistaken. Mother Teresa once said that abortions had opened us up to this insidious state of affairs in our society. Something to think about that is for sure. She had remarked that we had become a "culture of death."

"You May Have it With You"

My flight from Connecticut to California one year turned out to be a very lively one. At least three people came one after another to sit in the seat next to me throughout the flight. I was seated by the window and another passenger sat two seats away on the aisle. She was traveling together with a group from Maine and from time to time her friends would stop to chat. My reading material that day was Louis de Montford's, *Friends of the Cross*. It occurred to me that I should offer this wonderful little book to one of the ladies playing musical chairs. She eagerly accepted my invitation. After only a short period of time the woman turned to me and exclaimed, "You know, I've been searching for an answer to a particular problem in my life for three years, and I just found it in your book!"

Two women and myself were traveling together from Virginia to Omaha, Nebraska for a conference. When we walked down the aisle of the airplane a gentleman who was seated to the left of us greeted us very enthusiastically. During the course of our flight we entered into a conversation with him and he inquired if we were religious, since he felt that he could recognize a nun whenever he saw one. We told him, "No," but later I knew I had to ask him if he would like a rosary from Medjugorje, which I happened to have with me. Excitedly he exclaimed, "Yes," and proceeded to tell me that he had only recently returned from his wife's funeral in Mexico City where he had given his rosary to his mother-in-law. He was so excited by the thought of a replacement!

Once, I was seated next to a woman on an airplane who was animatedly sharing her life's story with me. She told me she had married someone of the Jewish faith and had converted from Catholicism to her husband's religion for the sake of their two sons. But since the boys were now grown, neither her nor her husband were actively involved with their faith. She did mention that her mom was a fervent Catholic. Undoubtedly, I had become too aggressive in my preaching to this lady, because if we had been sitting near an exit she would most assuredly have attempted to push me out of the airplane. In the midst of this turmoil I felt that it was necessary for me to offer her a Medjugorje rosary as well as another religious item, which I happened to have in my bag. Actually, I had to get up and walk to the other side of the airplane in order to obtain these items, since my husband was seated in another area and my luggage was with him. When I returned, she graciously accepted the gifts and said that her mom might be very pleased if she presented them to her.

By the end of our trip, she was once more in a good mood. As she left the airplane, she very sincerely said to me, "Keep up the good work!" The "good work" isn't always easy to keep up, Lord!

"Nothing to Fear but Fear Itself"

It was a quiet, peaceful summer afternoon. A gentle breeze drifted across my porch and stroked the meadow grasses which were interlaced with a multitude of wildflowers. You could not have found a more welcoming spot for contemplation. As I drifted off I entered what appeared to be a huge, dome-shaped building somewhere in the Middle East. When I opened the portal all that was visible was a wide expanse of green marble floor and, off in the distance, two heavy oak doors. This was the room which I knew I must enter. What greeted me on the other side was terrifying—a chamber full of slithering serpents, cobra snakes!

Snakes were always a personification of fear for me; particularly since some of my childhood encounters with them were extremely frightening. For instance, I once went to sit on a folding chair that I had just removed from our boathouse and a small garter snake slithered out between the crevices in the metal. For a young child who feared snakes this was a traumatic experience, particularly since I was alone. Another time I was walking amongst the sea grass close to the shore and stepped on a large water snake that squirmed out from under my bare feet. Then again, on another occasion I witnessed an enormous water snake swallowing an equally huge eel. It was a very disturbing sight!

In my vision I knew that I had no recourse but to walk through those reptiles in order to reach the heavy doors on the opposite side of the room. As I moved amongst the snakes, which were entwining themselves around my legs, I realized in retrospect that I could not feel their presence, even though I was able to see their bodies clearly. When I reached the doors on the other side of the room, two cobras faced me wrapped around the iron pulls, their hoods extended and mouths wide open. Since there was no other exit I had to grab the serpents around the neck in order to open the heavy doors. It was called do or die!

Once I stepped outside I was greeted by a gloriously beautiful garden with a dove cooing somewhere in the distance. As I opened my eyes out of the dream, I became aware of a dove sitting on a huge rock cooing in the meadow close to my porch. He then quickly flew away. What an experience! I felt that I had worked through some of my life's fears, which included a long phobia of snakes. At that particular period of my life I could not even look at a picture of a serpent without recoiling from the sight.

I retired early that night. Just as I was drifting into a deep sleep, I awakened, sat up in bed, and was confronted by a beautiful helmeted figure at the foot of my bed. The image was about a third of the size of a normal human being, clothed in royal robes, and held a staff in his hand with a snake entwined around its end. Much to my amazement, out of my mouth came, "I don't belong to you anymore!" With these words, the image vanished.

All we have to fear is fear itself. Fear of this sort does not come from God. Only Holy fear, which is that of not doing God's will. I evidently encountered Lucifer that night, a very beautiful fallen Archangel who usually presents himself in a much different form. I often wonder how I would have reacted if he had thrown the snake down on my bed!

Weeks later in Louisiana, my daughter Carol and I were looking for bamboo blinds in an import shop. While unrolling one of the shades to check it out for any imperfections, I became aware of a stuffed cobra snake mounted on a board with a mongoose very close by. The serpent's hood was extended in a striking position, and I knew that I had to reach out and grab the snake around its body. It wasn't easy; however, with God's help, I was able to do this. Thank You, Lord!

My husband and I decided to go to a carnival on a cool, breezy September evening in Dover, Delaware, where he happened to be stationed at the time. We were the only ones on the Ferris wheel that night when the operator suddenly walked away, leaving us swinging in the top of the wheel for at least twenty minutes. I happened to be pregnant with my son Chris, which made it even more terrifying. Needless to say, Ferris wheels were on my "hit list" ever after.

This was one of the fears I was called to face that summer. Afterwards, we were at a fair in New Hampshire, and the Ferris wheel was beckoning to me. I knew God did not want me to say, "No." I had to say, "Yes" and know that everything would be fine. He definitely gave me the courage to confront my fear. As a result, I enjoyed the experience immensely, just as I always had before my panic attack years ago.

That summer I also faced my fear of body surfing in ocean waves. After a frightening experience in Rehoboth Beach, Delaware, I developed a definite fear. I was tossed on my head by a huge wave and felt myself being carried out to sea by the undertow. I had to force myself to say, "Yes" to facing ocean waves once again.

Likewise, horseback riding was never a delight for me either, neither as a child nor as an adult. However, my daughter and her friends were going on a mountain trail ride in New Hampshire and I opted to join them.

All of these happenings were simply a piece of the puzzle necessary to give me the courage to say, "Yes" to other events in my life, which were yet to take place. You need to stretch that courage muscle, just as you do physical muscles.

By the way, in future years I even developed a friendship with a garter snake I named Charlie. He would come daily to sun himself on our doorstep in New Hampshire. You've come a long way baby! Thanks to You, Lord!

"Lock It or Leave It"

After my roommate and I had arrived at our hotel room in Mexico City, it occurred to me that I should check the locks on our accommodation's door. A close inspection revealed that the dead bolt did not fasten into anything, even though it appeared to do so. The screws on the chain lock were loose and could easily be removed from the wood by only a slight tug. This was quite a revelation for two ladies on a pilgrimage to Our Lady of Guadalupe Shrine, who had never encountered circumstances quite as blatant as this in the past. Since this was my roommate's first trip out of the States, she found the situation very frightening. I had experienced other strange circumstances in my travels, but nothing quite this obvious. It took four trips to the hotel manager to finally get our locks secured. Rigged hotel rooms are here to stay, if at all possible!

Many years later I had a most interesting conversation with an Indian gentleman in Seattle who was the desk clerk at a motel where we were planning to spend the night. When I asked him how he liked Seattle, he uttered one word of explanation, "Corruption."

After settling into our room on the ground floor and doing my praying, I felt God was telling me to check the window. To my surprise, it was not locked. You could slide it back approximately twelve inches before a screw in the window frame prevented any further opening.

Obviously, no one could crowd through this small space, but the locks on the door were very accessible to any-one who chose to reach through the opening and release the bolts. My husband and I found it was impossible for one person to be able to secure this bent window with a badly twisted fastener. After struggling with all of our strength, we were able to fix the obviously rigged room.

Around 1:00 in the morning, I was awakened by incredible activity on the second floor above us. At the same time I also heard excited voices coming from outside our window. Maybe some individuals who had thoughts of "corruption" in mind that night were thwarted? It def-initely was an intriguing speculation!

I have been in places such as Portugal where my balcony door lock was not working properly. Initially, I was not overly concerned. However, afterwards when I was in Yugoslavia, a lady in the room next to me awak-ened one night to find three men in her room. As a result, I decided it was a good idea to always report doors that did not close properly, particularly if I was going to be the sole occupant.

When I was in a hotel room in Rome, I left my light on all night because it seemed very possible that someone could come through the door while I slept. I did a lot of praying that evening. Father exclaimed the next morning, "I couldn't sleep all night because I was convinced someone was going to come into my room." It's a good thing to listen to your spirit when you feel there is a danger afoot unless you are someone who is particularly fearful of all unfamiliar situations.

While traveling in the States, my husband did have money stolen from his "locked" hotel room. Say those prayers, folks, and be cautious. God takes care of us.

Likewise, my stay in a large, busy motel located on an interstate highway near the Fatima Shrine in New Jersey was an exciting one. The adjoining room doors were locked only with small cabinet fasteners. A good jerk would definitely have taken care of any security that they provided. As I tried desperately to get to sleep, I was entertained by great activity in one of the rooms next door. Prostitutes were soliciting truck drivers. Drug transactions were taking place, and who knows what else? Fear washed over me as I lay there. Should I pack my bag and leave? I opted not to and eventually all activity ceased. Thank You, Lord!

Later, in another country, I would have left my room because of similar circumstances, but in retrospect, it would not have been prudent to do so. Just as in New Jersey, staying and trusting was the name of the game. We must try to discern what action God is asking from us at the moment, then take it or leave it!

"Ride at Your Own Risk"

$\mathcal{All}$ modes of transportation in India can be memorable. For instance, when I was in Calcutta, India, riding in a taxicab was a thrilling experience. The driver would put his foot on the gas and his hand on the horn as he competed aggressively with busses, motorcycles, cows, cars, rickshaws, etc... for the right of way. During these experiences, if you had forgotten how to pray, it was a great time to refresh your memory!

When we were in India, my friend Lou was told that if you were ever in an accident, you'd better get out and run for your life. The crowds would kill you as well as the driver if they could catch you. We were never sure that this was a fact, until I questioned an airline pilot's wife whose husband flew to India. I was told that this was absolutely true. While speaking to a fourth grade class a while later, I mentioned this reality about taxis in Calcutta. A young Indian student very matter-of-factly stated, "They would sell the body parts and buy a house." Amen!

Likewise, riding in a bus was also a very memorable experience in India. Watch out world! The driver is separated from the rest of humanity by a grate across his area, no doubt for protection from the wall of humanity usually present. One day when we attempted to board the vehicle, I thought that I would end up having to ride standing on the outside steps hanging onto the railing, just like you see in the movies. Lou was not going to allow that to happen if she could possibly help it. She pulled me into a bus which looked as though it could not possibly hold another soul.

Riding in a rickshaw was not something we ever wished to do either. However, on several occasions we had no alternative. It was an experience that left you feeling death cold possibly be waiting around the next corner. I told my friend Lou that if we died in such a manner, it did have some value. How many folks could say that their mother or grandmother died in a rickshaw in Calcutta? That has to be worth something!

One day we could not locate a cab, so we used a rickshaw whose driver kept hounding us until we agreed to be his passengers. As we simultaneously attempted to seat ourselves, our fannies became wedged so that we were not able to fully sit down. It was rather like being suspended in mid-air, and the driver took off before we were properly situated. We were laughing hysterically as we clutched the sides of the rickshaw to keep from being thrown out. The poor man did not understand English and must have felt that we were laughing at him. After navigating a traffic jam, he suddenly stopped in the middle of the street and motioned for us to leave. Sadly, we were not able to make him comprehend our dilemma. We knew he desperately needed the money since he had hounded us for our business. We were probably the only rickshaw customers in the history of Calcutta to be literally thrown out on the street!

"Lend It or Give It?"

While attending evangelization school in Florida, I became aware that the gentleman seated next to me reminded me of the person in my husband's and my life who, for many years, owed us a considerable amount of money. Not only did this individual have a similar outward appearance, but he also told me that he was in the exact same business. God really wanted me to search my heart for any unforgiveness that I may have had toward this man. Lord, please remove any anger or hatred that may be present!

Every year, at least once for the past seven years, we have received a phone call from the gentleman announcing that the check was in the mail or it would be on its way in a matter of weeks. Promises, promises, but no check in sight! There have been a few small ones but not the full money owed.

The Bible says that when you lend, you give. This was the only reason my husband had not taken legal action against this individual. In January of last year, I had received a phone call from our "friend" and much to my amazement I did not feel any negative emotion of which I was aware.

The church where we attended Mass in Florida had another gentle reminder underfoot. There were the same unique ceramic tiles in the church that our builder had installed in the home he had constructed for us. The school I was attending suggested you bake your "adversary" a cake. Interestingly enough, when I returned home there was a check in the mail from the builder for $200.

God does throw us a bone from time to time. Was this individual aiding or abetting my (our) entrance into heaven? This was the question. Forgive and be forgiven is what we say in the Lord's Prayer. Do we really understand, or do we choose not to? Lord, it's not easy, but you forgive me daily for my sins. When I ask for forgiveness, please give me the grace to forgive others!

"Dogs Come and Dogs Go"

Suki was a German shepherd we purchased as a puppy in New Hampshire. It was a birthday gift for our 14-year-old daughter, Sarah. When we chose Suki out of the three remaining puppies from a litter of seven, the lady told us she knew nothing about this particular dog. As Suki grew older I became aware that when you looked into her eyes, she was unfathomable. There was definitely an unreachable part of this animal, a touch of the wild, which absolutely proved to be true. Living in Connecticut at the time, we had many deer in our area. Suki, we discovered, had become the leader of a pack of dogs that chased deer. She would sneak out of the house and leave the property at every possible opportunity. Although I took her in the car with me during the cooler part of the year, it was not possible during the warmer months.

The night before Sarah was to leave as an exchange student for New Zealand, I received a phone call from a neighbor who told me Suki had just attacked her dog as she walked through our neighborhood. The lady was very upset by Suki's aggressive behavior. Thankfully, her animal was not wounded, but certainly could have been. This was in the early part of June, and my husband and I were leaving for a trip to North Carolina the day after Sarah's departure. Dick, our son home from college for the summer, was working full-time and had a girlfriend, Lisa, who lived in the New York area. After his job ended for the day, he would often immediately head for Lisa's house without returning home. Therefore, Suki would be confined and totally unsupervised for a large period of time. A vet once told me, if you pen up a German shepherd, you were asking for trouble.

Unfortunately, buried electrical fences were not in use to any extent in our area. My only alternative seemed to be to get rid of this dog; an action I knew would not be well accepted by Sarah upon her return at the end of the summer. The Westport pound, in a neighboring town, was a very popular place for local people to acquire their pets. I knew many individuals who had obtained great animals there. After Mass that morning I asked Father to please pray and see if he felt that I was doing the right thing. It was a most difficult decision for me to make since I also liked Suki. However, Father agreed that Suki must go and the place I mentioned seemed to be the answer.

It turned out that Sarah was very disturbed by my decision upon her return from New Zealand. I knew that I had caused her a great deal of pain. Fortunately, on Christmas Eve while waiting at a stoplight, a car pulled up next to her with Suki and a small child in the backseat. Suki became extremely excited when she saw her. Sarah, in turn, wept as Suki recognized her and jumped around in the vehicle. That Christmas, Sarah's special gift from God was the knowledge that Suki was alive and situated in a loving family. Subsequently, the following year, Sarah left for college, and we moved to a condo in Virginia. God's timing was painful, but perfect, because Suki would have had to go sooner or later.

"Our Lady's Presence"

I first encountered a green silhouette of the Blessed Mother on my trip to Medjugorje, Yugoslavia, in 1985. She presented herself to me in the area where she first appeared to the children in 1981. On this same pilgrimage one of the ladies on our pilgrimage took a picture of me beside the big stone cross on Mt. Krizevac seated next to another member of our group. When she sent me the photo, I was amazed to see a brilliant green light by my side. To my knowledge, there was nothing visibly present which could have produced such an image. Many times, since my initial vision, I have been aware of the Blessed Mother's presence by the appearance of a green light.

My husband and I were driving from Oklahoma to Arizona when we decided to stop in Lubbock, Texas, where the Blessed Mother supposedly was appearing. As we entered the church for Mass that day, I was aware of a green light, which clearly indicated to me the Virgin Mary's presence. Shortly before Father gave his homily, he was interrupted by a policeman who announced that they had received a call saying a bomb had been planted somewhere in the church complex. After relating this bit of information to the congregation, Father continued with his sermon. We all sat there until were ordered by the police to remove ourselves from the building and proceed to the courtyard. The thought, which occurred to me at the time, was, "If you have to die, what better place than the church to do so!" They never located a bomb, but it did make for a thought-provoking afternoon!

When I visited the Shrine of Our Lady of Czestochowa in Poland, our pilgrimage group was very blessed to be close to the icon of the Blessed Mother. She smiled at me. What a great gift!

"Human Beings, Trash or Treasure?"

While I attended a religious seminar with my daughter Carol in Louisiana, we were told by the priest, who happened to be the lecturer, that if women had more education concerning this issue, abortion could be totally eradicated. I heartily disagreed and without thinking made the comment, b___s___ to Carol who was seated next to me. It was incredible that Father heard my remark, because we were seated in the back of the classroom. The only other person, besides the lecturer, who was aware of my comment, was the gentleman seated directly in front of me. God had to have wanted the instructor to know that his comment was total nonsense. The thought of having to qualify his statement made him extremely agitated, and he angrily remarked to me, "What you said was totally uncalled for!" With this announcement, he packed up his books and left the classroom. I apologized to Father for my crude remark, but the class was at a lost to understand exactly what had transpired. Since he vanished without a word of explanation to anyone, it was up to me to inform them as to what had provoked Father's abrupt departure, a most humiliating experience.

We need to understand how to know, love, and serve God. This is the knowledge we must have in order

to eradicate abortion. Education without being God cen-
tered cannot be the answer. The reality of the fetus being
a human being, no matter how small, has to be recognized from the time of conception. He or she has been
made in the image and likeness of God. This has to be
realized in the depths of our spirit and not just our heads.
We know that at the moment of conception, the potential
for a complete human being is present. It is all there.

Some of the most "educated" people I know have
been involved with abortion. We have to understand its
murder we're committing and simply not getting rid of
an inconvenience in our lives. "This is my body, and I'm
in charge" is a ridiculous assumption because the baby is
a separate human being. In the case of rape, it is not justi-
fiable to kill the child for the sin of the father. Remember,
we did not create this child, and therefore it is not for us
to destroy what God has made. Being in a mother's
womb today can be a most dangerous place!

My daughter Sarah, a nurse, had a very unsettling
experience in the emergency room one night. A lady
came in who was in the midst of aborting a three month-
old baby. While she was using the lavatory, the baby was
expelled, and Sarah was one of those responsible for
cleaning up afterwards. When she went to remove the
child from the floor, the baby moved its arm! There could
not have been a stronger indication of the reality of this
being a human being than what occurred that evening.
As a result, Sarah came home the next morning visibly
shaken by her experience because, in the past, she had
been uncertain of what she truly believed as far as abortion was concerned.

We have been asked to pray daily for a baby whose mother may be contemplating an abortion, even to the extent of giving it a name. A friend told me a very interesting story concerning a couple that she knew who wished to adopt a child. They were faithfully praying for a baby who might become a victim of abortion. When they were offered a newborn for adoption, they were astounded to hear that its name was the same as the one they had been praying for in it's mother's womb— Richard Christopher!

When pregnant with my first child, I met a lady who was likewise pregnant but with her third. However, it was the first baby to be born to her and her second husband. She had two beautiful daughters who were offspring's of her previous marriage. Openly she expressed to all that she did not want this child. When the baby, a perfectly healthy boy, was born dead, the doctors could not find any medical explanation for its death. How tough can God be with our unbelief—a trash or a treasure?

"Creative Crosses"

While in India, my friend Lou and I worked with small children. They had either been abandoned by their parents or brought to the sisters because they were near death from starvation. There was one small child in particular who was suffering from extreme malnutrition and never gave any sign of being aware of her surroundings. This changed, however, when one evening while I was bending over her bed, she reached out to touch the cross which hung around my neck. It was a very special moment for me as well as the first sign of her road to recovery.

While my husband and I traveled from New Hampshire to Connecticut, I became aware of a variety of crosses in the sky, which lasted for many miles. The cloud formations were quite extraordinary. Since we were on our way to baby-sit for our grandsons, I remarked to my husband, "This is going to be a most interesting week." Believe me, it was! The ten-month old Noah and my husband were ill during this time. It was definitely an agony and ecstasy experience.

On an Ash Wednesday in Calcutta, India, I was extremely ill. From 12:00 noon until 3:00 in the afternoon my thirst was incredible. There was no boiled water available at this time. I knew this must have been what Jesus experienced on the cross; however, His thirst was for our souls and not really for water.

My real cross, without redemptive value, comes when I cross my will with His will and I refuse to surrender myself to Him. By the way, the people whom I have met who hate the word "suffering" are those who seemingly suffer the most. As human beings we are going to suffer. However, if we refuse to offer this suffering to God for the love of Him, then it will be a truly agonizing experience. But if we offer it up to God to save souls, then maybe the suffering will be more joyful than painful.

"The Bolder, the Better"

While packing up one morning in Arizona to
drive back to Idaho I had another exciting key adventure.
After putting my belongings in the car, I returned to the
house for any over-looked possessions. Unfortunately,
when I returned to my vehicle it was securely locked with
my keys, purse, and all my money sitting on the front
seat.

Since my daughter and granddaughter were both
unreachable at this time of the day, I called the police to
see if they were willing to open my car, an action the gentleman at the Toyota dealership recommended. They
informed me that they no longer performed such duties.
The Toyota people could make me another key, but I had
to obtain a key code number for them from the dealer
where the automobile was originally purchased.
Unfortunately the dealership happened to be back in
Idaho. When I called information to obtain the number, I
realized I had completely forgotten their exact name.
Therefore, I requested the operator check the yellow
pages for a Toyota dealership in the area. Thankfully, she
was graciously willing to do so. Finally, she found a number and gave it to me. Once I contacted the dealership
they said they would call me back with the key code. The
next problem to be solved was how was I going to get to

the local car dealer when I had no money for a cab? There was no cash to be found anywhere in the house.

The taxi had to be the answer since the Toyota dealership in Scottsdale was much too far from our house for me to be able to walk to their place of business. When the driver responded to my call, I explained to him that I had no money to pay him because my wallet was locked in the car. I was also bold enough to ask if he would be willing to lend me the cash for a new car key. Fortunately, he was an older cab driver who seemingly was very understanding of forgetful old ladies. After patiently waiting for me to have the key made, he drove back to the house in time for me to leave Arizona before noon.

I must say that God has made me extremely bold in my old age. There is always a solution to a problem if you keep praying like crazy and trusting beyond reason. The big glitch is to not let it upset you! Keep peaceful! God is in control and all is well. Thank You, Lord!

"Who am I?"

God chose to place an individual in my life who was like a mirror of me. I was in my forties during the late sixties, with five teenager's, two babies, and a husband who was a corporate pilot absent from home most of the time. My sugar addiction had reached great heights at this point in my life; therefore, Overeaters Anonymous (OA) was my salvation. Working through the fourth step was a revelation to me. It's easy to see everyone else's humanity, but not so easy to recognize your personal faults and virtues. As human beings, we all have the same ingredients. You may have more of this or less of that than I, but hopefully, sometime in our life we become aware that it's all there in each one of us. "Who am I?" is the question. It can be pretty scary to find out, but very freeing at the same time. The truth will set you free! Once I acknowledged it in myself, I could have cared less if you saw it in me.

I was at a prayer meeting where a friend said to me, "You could talk to a fire hydrant!" After mentioning this remark to an acquaintance, she responded, "And the fire hydrant would probably talk back!" Several weeks later at another meeting a lady spoke up and announced that she could talk to a fire hydrant. What occurred to me after she said this was that we would both tell the fire hydrant exactly what we wanted it to know and nothing more. People who chatter a lot often use the same tactics as someone who seldom speaks at all. We are definitely controlling how near we allow people to get to us. Only after I have acknowledged something exists within myself do I feel comfortable with others being aware of its presence in me.

Very often I would recognize one of those ingredients in myself and I would see my friend acting it out. However, it was fine because I really liked this person. He had faults and idiosyncrasies very similar to mine. While sitting in church for morning Mass one day, God said to me, "Nancy, don't you understand? You love yourself." (Hopefully not narcissistic love but one of acceptance as He accepts us.) If I could love this human being who mirrored me, then what I was saying was that I loved myself. What a revelation that was!

After Mass I went to Caldor's and while shopping had a strange gentleman remark to me, "You certainly are sailing around today!" Indeed I was. It was a whole new world!

"Calcutta, Ready or Not!"

Early in the morning of the day we were to depart for Calcutta, I received a phone call from my friend Lou who told me she had no money for the trip. It happened to be Martin Luther King Day and all the banks in Massachusetts were closed. Her only alternative was to collect her friends' ATM cards in order to obtain as much cash as possible. As we stood in the wrong line in the airport in Germany, I made the statement to her that we didn't have a full brain between the two of us. Hopefully, Calcutta was ready. However, Sister did write to me back in the States after returning from our trip and mentioned that Calcutta was never the same after we left.

In the Kennedy Airport we encountered a Father who was on his way to India to give a retreat to Mother Teresa's Sisters. It was great to have someone accompanying us who was as inexperienced as we were. Back in Virginia I did not feel called to gather any information concerning my trip to Calcutta; however, God apparently had something else in mind. While attending a New Year's retreat weekend in Virginia Beach, I was greeted by the book, *City of Joy*, as I entered the door. When I questioned the person in charge as to why this book about Calcutta was there, he responded that he didn't really know. The retreat weekend had nothing do with

India and was totally out of context. He added that he simply had grabbed it out of his bookcases as he left the house that morning. The shocking pink cover of *City of Joy* was hard to miss, and the contents were equally as shocking for someone without any third world experience. I had no choice but to read this book. Thank You, Lord! It was a great preparation for our life to come.

We were extremely fortunate to have hooked up with Father, because when the Sisters met him at the airport, he requested they give us a ride into town. As we were driving Sister asked us if we'd like to work with them at their Dum-Dum compound. She said that we would be provided with a bed and food in exchange for our services. We agreed to do this and thoroughly enjoyed taking care of small children who had either been abandoned or brought to them because of malnutrition.

Every day was extremely abrasive for anyone coming into such an unfamiliar culture. Not even the Indians go to Calcutta if they can help it. The noise level was incredible with horns blowing, crows cawing, rats squealing, and music blaring over loudspeakers day and night during their holidays. We arrived in the midst of their Independence Day celebration, and during these days, music sounded continuously. There are approximately 300 Indian holidays a year, which makes for great, noisy festivities. Adding to the chaos, the crows were very determined critters and would steal food from any dish the moment you turned your back. We fed the children outdoors on the patio; therefore, it was a continual battle with these birds. The room where we slept was located next to the area where the mentally retarded people were housed, and often at night I would be awakened by screams coming from someone having a nightmare. Making the setting even more unique was the fact that there were no screens on the windows. We had to be very sure that our mosquito netting was securely tucked in every evening. Likewise, no one could drink the water unless it had been boiled for twenty minutes. Since diesel fuel was used in all vehicles and cow dung burned for cooking purposes and heat, the air pollution was incredible. Because the sun heated the water, showers were usually an afternoon affair. If you spent twenty minutes or more outside, your nostrils were filled with soot. Lou said she coughed up black stuff out of her lungs for a year after our return to the States.

Making our experience in India even more memorable was driving in their taxis. I did the praying and my friend Lou did the paying. She handled our finances beautifully despite the hassling that went on from time to time with the taxi driver or local merchants. The most important thing for us to do during our trip was to look for Jesus in everyone and to stay as positive as possible in every situation. There were too many opportunities to go "down the aluminum tube." After practicing this attitude faithfully for a month, I was able to return to the States with great acceptance for others, particularly my family. Unfortunately, some of that wore off as time went by. It was not a matter of survival as it was in India.

Fortunately for us, Mother Teresa was most accessible to us at the Mother House in Calcutta, and we were very blessed to see her quite often. We took a picture with her, which when developed showed me in a misty atmosphere surrounded by rainbow lights. Someone remarked that it looked as though I were encased in raw cotton. When we were talking one day about being in the Immaculate Heart of Mary and the Sacred Heart of Jesus, it suddenly occurred to me that this is what had taken place in Calcutta. By the way, Mother Teresa told us that she hated to have her picture taken, so she made a deal with God that every time she consented to do so, He would release a soul from Purgatory.

All my experience in India was filtered. This is exactly what the Blessed Mother is trying to tell us all to do. Put yourself in the Immaculate Heart of Mary and the Sacred Heart of Jesus for protection, healing, and conversion. I can vouch for it being a very safe place. You will undergo all that others will encounter, but it will not be in the same intensity.

Calcutta was an experience of a lifetime, as well as preparation for a lifestyle that could possibly await us in the United States. It was my Outward Bound adventure!

"Pick It Up or Pass It By?"

There was a time in my life when I felt called to pick up hitchhikers. One particular gentleman, whose car had broken down, asked me why I was giving him a lift. "How come you're giving me a ride when you're definitely not the type to pick up people along the road?" It seemed as though God was asking me to trust Him enormously at this particular stage in my spiritual walk. Who knows? I sometimes make the remark that I can see God saying, "Look at that nut! She thinks this is what I want her to do!" However, if He truly loves us and knows we are trying to please Him, I believe He does honor our intentions.

The only time I ever had anything unfortunate happen to me concerning hitchhikers was when a friend asked me to give a male acquaintance of one of her children a ride from Annapolis to New York. During that trip I lost my checkbook.

A lady whom I picked up to take to work one day had a very sad story. She had lost her car right before Christmas and desperately needed money to buy gifts for her two children. It was obvious that God wanted me to provide the means for this unhappy lady to be able to give here kids a joyful holiday.

While traveling from Annapolis, Maryland, to Connecticut, I stopped to pick up a young woman who was hitchhiking near the Chesapeake Bay Bridge. As she was telling me her destination, a male companion, who had been well hidden when I stopped, opened the back door and hopped into the car. I then told them that I needed a minute to rethink the situation. Maybe I was not offering either one of them a ride after all. Was I willing to take these two to the New Jersey Turnpike where they could proceed to their destination in Atlantic City? I did consent to do this and had a most interesting trip. The hitchhikers turned out to be two German students who had been touring the States during their summer vacation and were now returning home. Actually, they had partic-ipated in a protest rally in San Francisco. From what they said they did this sort of thing frequently in Germany. The girl firmly believed that you could bring about change through violence, while her male companion expressed otherwise. He felt peaceful means were a bet-ter approach for transformation. I had a friend who once told me that his family in another country was devoted to keeping peace. What entered my mind was, "If you don't stay peaceful, I'll kill you!" This was not the answer to bringing about peace. Peace comes only from loving God and neighbor. It comes from within and is the result of letting go of all unforgiveness of self and others. This, thereby, allows God to fill us with His peace.

When the time came for me not to pick up hitch-hikers anymore, I had a most interesting experience. There, standing along the road in New Hampshire, was a rather unsavory looking character. I passed him by but then had second thoughts on the matter. After I prayed about whether or not I needed to turn around and offer him a ride, I believed the answer was, "Yes." What a sur-prise awaited me when I returned to get him. He was now on the opposite side of the road headed west instead of east! This was a very fitting climax to my hitchhiker experiences. Today, I'm rarely aware of a hitchhiker, and when I am, I do not feel called to action. I say a prayer for them and continue on my way. It was a piece of the puz-zle which was obviously for a particular time and place—just not the present.

"Stuff is for Stuffing"

Things can never make us truly happy. We are forever convincing ourselves that if our circumstances were different, such as having a different job, more money, a bigger house in a better location, or a different physical appearance, then we would be happy. If only I was a "somebody," then others would have more respect for me as a person, and I would have better feelings about myself.

What fools we mortals are! Only God can give us joy and peace. It is grace and strictly a result of loving God enough that enables us to relinquish our will for His will. My will is the only gift I have to give to the Almighty. It is through this act of love that we receive what we seek.

In the Air Force, there were folks whom we would meet who were always miserable wherever they happened to be stationed. Their song and dance routine was that the last place of duty was great, and retirement would be utopia because they would then have everything their hearts desired. All of this was absolute nonsense, since we knew them back when they were at their last duty station. They were just as unhappy as they were in their present location. Life is never perfect, but we do have a choice of looking at the bottle and determining if it is half-empty or half-full. It's our choice, an act of will, to accentuate the positive or the negatives. We need to know that everything that happens to us has a purpose in our lives. It is a piece of the puzzle that is neither good nor bad. In retrospect, we see from what was considered a disaster at the time, came great good. If God truly loves us, He isn't going to allow anything to happen that is not for growth in our relationship with Him. As humans, we love to terrorize ourselves as well as others. God is a lover, not a terrorist!

There is a definite connection between stuff on the outside and stuff on the inside. If we have an inordinate attachment to our possessions, this will fill up our inner space leaving little room for God. Human beings have an incredible love affair with their dead relatives' belongings that they have inherited. It can cause great dissension in a family as to who gets what after a family member's death. If you want to do everyone a great favor, get rid of it all. They may be angry with you as a result, but at least not with each other. At that point in time, you could care less, I'm sure!

I was a great collector of stuff at one period of my life. Junk shops, garage sales, dumps, and garbage cans were my feeding places. When we moved from Connecticut to Virginia after my husband's retirement, I knew it all had to go. If I wished to get to the next step in my life, I had to let go of the one I was on. It was not possible to straddle the two. There is no way we could have moved around the way we have, if I had still been attached to my possessions. My time on pilgrimages would have been divided between God and stuff (too many cheap goodies to be had overseas). God would certainly have been left wanting!

Wherever I have lived, I have always loved the location as well as the home. Much work went in to these dwellings to make them uniquely ours, and it was not easy to pack up and leave after we had achieved what, at times, seemed like the impossible. "It's mine and I love it, but it's time to say farewell." It is not easy to say, "yes" but it is extremely rewarding in the end. I know from past experience, there is always something else equally wonderful on the horizon. If it's His Will, trust Him. He will always provide beautifully!

"To Live or to Die"

There have been moments in my life when I truly believed that I had to make a decision as to whether I chose to live or to die.

One particular incident occurred when we were spending our vacation in Rehoboth Beach, Delaware, where body surfing was an exciting pastime for most members of our family. Since I had been raised near the relatively calm water of the Chesapeake Bay, I always had a passion for water sports, but not those associated with powerful ocean waves. My husband, who came from the Virginia Beach area, felt perfectly at home with strong ocean currents. This particular afternoon the kids and I were having a wonderful time in the surf when suddenly a huge wave came and flipped me onto my head and propelled me into the sandy ocean bottom. Stunned and disoriented by the blow, I found myself being swept out to sea by a strong undertow. At this moment, it would have been easy to give into the peaceful lethargic feeling that overwhelmed me, but my survival instincts took over and I struggled back to shore. I emerged from the surf badly shaken with my head and shoulder bleeding profusely. Other than being slightly dizzy, I was fine.

Another life or death decision of mine became apparent during the birth of my sixth child. It was 3:00 a.m. when I arrived at the local Air Force Base Hospital more than ready to have my baby. I purposely chose to wait until my labor pains had increased since, my labors had always been long and drawn out. I was hoping that this one would be different. After the doctor examined me, he announced that it would not be long before I would give birth. I was then wheeled into the delivery room. Unfortunately, I allowed him to talk me into having a saddle block to stop the pain, which subsequently stopped labor immediately. As a result, he then decided to induce labor with pitocin, a drug that was administered intravenously. Almost immediately after he started to administer the drug, he and the nurse left for an emergency elsewhere in the hospital. They left me unattended for almost two hours! Hard labor resumed within minutes of their departure to such an extent that I soon became exhausted from the severe uninterrupted contractions. As this excruciatingly painful experience continued with no relief in sight and no one to help me, I felt like simply giving up. However, I knew instinctively that if I did so, neither the baby nor I would survive. I had learned afterwards that after multiple pregnancies the uterus becomes thinly stretched and therefore can easily rupture. Suddenly the nurse appeared and announced that my baby was coming. "Hold it until the doctor arrives!" she exclaimed. That was definitely a night to remember!

Thanksgiving morning, after visiting my friend Lou, I headed for home in my Volkswagen Bug with several of her kids as well as mine in the car. As we drove towards my house, it occurred to me that this would be a great time to visit the local dump. At this period of my life I was still into junk in a big way. We entered a very deserted garbage heap, but found no "goodies" amongst the trash. As we started to leave and drove towards the main entrance, I became aware of two strange men who had parked their car and were in the process of closing the gate on us, trapping us in! The serious look on their faces led me to believe that this was not a joking matter. By the determined expression on my face, they knew that I did not intend to stop no matter what. At the last possible moment before I could crash into the gate, they opened it and allowed us to escape. Obviously, we were trespassing on their territory!

This dump was a trash-picker's paradise. A lot of money was made from good stuff that these people were able to rescue before the bulldozer would come. No one would have thought of looking for our bodies at the dump! Sometimes you just know it's time for action and you'd better take it! God saves, but he who hesitates may be lost!

"Our Lord, Our Life"

It was during Mass one Ash Wednesday when I asked God what I should give up for Lent. I was afraid that maybe it would be sugar, because I am a sugar addict and it was always a sacrifice for me to overcome my sweet tooth. The answer I received was shocking. It was "everything." I was to subsist only on Eucharist and water for forty days! My friend Elaine, who had sat next to me during the sacrifice of the Mass, asked me as we left the church, "What on earth happened to you during the service?" When I told her about God's request, she had as much difficulty dealing with it as I did. My husband, understandably, was equally horrified. He gave his consent, but only under the condition that if he saw a difference in my ability to function I was to stop immediately. I agreed to Speight's request because if there was a change in my capability to carry out my normal everyday activities, I knew that God was not sustaining me. As a result, it would not be His wish for me to continue.

During these fasts, (there was more than one), I was able to function normally. I performed all my daily duties as wife and grandmother, baby-sat three children for a daughter who went overseas, drove myself from Virginia to Connecticut during an emergency, went on a vacation, and entertained, (which was actually a treat since I enjoyed preparing food for others). My husband declared that he had never eaten so well. It turned out that no one was aware of my fasting unless my husband, or someone who happened to know me, informed them. I lost weight but otherwise did not show any signs of physical deterioration.

An Indian doctor, very familiar with starvation, examined me thoroughly after my first forty day fast. He announced that other than a weight loss, he could find no signs or symptoms normally associated with malnutrition.

The amazing thing was that God allowed me to eat normally immediately after the fast ended, never having any ill affects. A nutritionist afterwards explained to me that if you were to eat solid foods immediately after fasting for such a long period of time, your body would have a very difficult time functioning.

There is no doubt in my mind that God can perform miracles through the Eucharist. It is His Body. It is His blood. We must surrender totally to God's Will. Your Will and not our will be done.

"Who Wants a Broken Leg?"

My husband and I had just dropped our New Zealand exchange student off at Kennedy airport in New York. Anna was a guest of ours in Connecticut for six months where she attended school with our daughter Sarah, who previously had spent three months as an exchange student in New Zealand. We were discussing what an eventful year 1987 had been thus far when my husband made the remark that after thirty-nine years he was tired of all of the leadership responsibilities at work. Having been in a very serious automobile accident in February, which destroyed his left hip, he found the long work hours of a corporate pilot extremely stressful. Sarah was entering college in September; therefore, he felt that retirement was out of the question for the moment.

That Saturday afternoon two friends and myself left for Brooklyn, New York, to hear Mother Teresa, who was speaking at one of the local Catholic Churches. After her talk she announced to the audience that she was praying for all of our families.

My friends and I enjoyed a very exciting face-to-face encounter with Mother Teresa. As she left the church that afternoon, she gave each of us a special blessing which was a wonderful unexpected gift from God.

As I entered our driveway, my two sons, who were in the car with their father, were heading toward the main street. My initial thought was, "Goody, we're all going to dinner." When they saw me, Dick jumped out of the car, ran up to my window and announced that they were on their way to the hospital. He told me that Dad had lost his memory. Apparently he was exercising at the gym when he started to lose it. Although he was able to find his way home, he could remember little else. God is good.

Three months before Speight's "happening," a neighbor of ours had a similar incident occur. In fact, a friend called me one Sunday asking me to pray for him. I encountered this gentleman at church only a few days before my husband's experience and was told all about his transient-global amnesia, which is what this malady has been medically labeled. Businessmen traveling abroad, over stressed, would arrive at their destination with a total memory loss. The memory does return, but as the doctor explained, if stress continues, this may reoccur. My husband returned to normal around 9:00 that evening; however, he was never able to remember what took place during that brief memory lapse. Subsequently, extensive tests showed no other physical ailments were responsible for his loss. Stress was the only culprit.

God and Mother Teresa's prayers took care of my husband's desire not to remain in his work leadership role. As a result, they also removed him from the possibility of losing his memory during a future flight.

A friend reminded me that I had once said, "If a shepherd has a sheep that refuses to listen and continues to wander off, in desperation, he will break the lamb's leg." My husband refused to listen to any of us at that time. He desperately needed to slow down, but he chose to ignore our pleas for a change in lifestyle.

God can be speaking to us often through others. No one wants a broken leg. Do we? He definitely has a way of getting our attention. Just remember everything has a purpose. My husband soon afterwards retired. He later made the statement that after retirement came the best days of his life. There was time for his family, for things he always wanted to do, and most importantly, time for God.

"Listen to the Improbable"

Our head will absolutely not tell us what God is asking us to do, or not to do. It can give as many reasons for taking a particular course of action as it can for not doing so. Discernment of God's will comes from the heart. There were times in my life where it was very clearly shown to me that what God was asking defied all reasoning. If I had followed through on what my heart told me, things would have worked out; however, I chose not to be obedient and then paid the price.

One example of this disobedience, as a result of not listening, developed when my husband was returning from a trip on the East Coast. He planned to arrive at Idaho Falls on an 11:30 a.m. flight from Salt Lake City. He phoned to say that his connection in Ohio was going to be one hour late; therefore, I naturally assumed this would affect his entire flight schedule. I tried to get in touch with the airlines concerning the change in his arrival but they could not provide me with any further information. In praying about this dilemma, I got, "Go down to meet the flight as previously planned." Unfortunately, since my head kept saying that this was nonsense, I foolishly listened to my head and not my heart. I rationalized that an hour late flight could not make a connection with a flight that was to leave at the exact same time as their scheduled arrival time. Because we lived an hour away from Idaho Falls I did not want to make an unnecessary trip. It was a four-hour wait between flights from Salt Lake City at this time of the day. As a result, I waited 45 minutes past the designated time at home, hoping that maybe the Utah flight would be late taking off so my husband could make his originally scheduled flight.

Once I arrived at the airport there was no sign of my husband. I was told that the airplane came in as planned but Speight Drummond was not on the manifest. I decided that I would have to waste time in Idaho Falls until the next flight arrived. Fortunately for both of us, I needed to use the restroom before leaving the airport. As I opened the door, I happened to glance towards the small terminal restaurant whose customers could not be clearly seen from the rest of the airport lobby. There sat my husband having lunch! He somehow had arrived on time. His wife had not. Needless to say, neither of us was happy with each other. Mad was actually more like it! God knows, I did not listen, listen, listen!

"Rosary at the Lake"

I told my granddaughter Lisa, that if it was not for the rosary, there was a good possibility that she would not be here. Her mom and dad at one time were having some marital difficulties as many of us have experienced in our lives; therefore, Carol was trying to decide what course of action she should take at that moment, if any. My family, at the time, was spending the month of August at our cottage in New Hampshire. There I would spend as much time as possible drifting serenely in a canoe on the wonderful Mountain Lake, while very often saying the rosary.

This particular afternoon I was praying for God's will to be done in my daughter's troubled situation. We had no telephone in our cottage at the time; consequently, we used the one in the small village nearby. I felt called to give Carol a ring later that day. She told me that a school in town had phoned her asking if she was interested in filling a teacher's position which had become available. Since classes were beginning shortly, they were desperate to find a replacement for a teacher who had just informed them she would not be able to fulfill her obligation for the coming year.

My daughter had lived in this small town only a short while. She was a teacher, but had never taught after receiving her degree and had never applied for a job.

Because there were three little ones at home, with no baby sitter and no clothes for working in the marketplace, she naturally said it was impossible for her to accept the offer. My immediate response was, "Call them back, and find out more about the job, and then tell them, YES."

This definitely was God's answer to my prayer. The thought was a terrifying one, and despite all my daughter's fears, she went for an interview and consented to accept the position. Miraculously, her sister was coming to graduate school in the area in a few days with money for her to buy clothes. In addition, a baby sitter came out of the wood-work, and both she and her husband chose a course of action that brought them much peace.

Interestingly enough, prior to all of this, when she was to graduate from the University of Maine with a teaching degree in December, they informed her at the last possible moment that she was lacking one course in order to receive her diploma. She was terribly upset by the announcement; however, when she moved down south, the first thing she knew she must do was to take the accreditation course for teaching in Louisiana and get her degree. Although she never, even for one moment, dreamed she would be using it so soon. Her returning to school was also the impetus for her husband to go back and finish his degree.

God puts it all together, if we wish to listen. Your will and not my will be done. Sometimes it is not easy, but good things are never easy!

"Claim It"

I had read an article about a man who was on an airplane that was about to crash. It was a very impressive story because he was the only survivor amongst 150 people who died in the terrible accident. Maintaining that God said He was taking care of him, he repeatedly "claimed it" and God honored this man's complete trust in His Word. He was saved. Relating this story to a fellow passenger who happened to be traveling with me on a pilgrimage, I was stunned by the ladies retort, "Oh yes, he moved three times on the plane before he was thrown out of the plane." Obviously she knew of him.

My own personal experiences with the phrase, "You said it Lord, now do it," was put to the test when I would fast. It was during a Palm Sunday vigil Mass that I felt as though I was going to pass out. I had to leave the church, stand outside, and claim the fact that He was taking care of me because after all, He said He was. This was the 40th day of my fast. If in fact I fainted and had to go to the hospital, how would such a nut be greeted? My husband maintained they would probably throw him in jail for allowing his wife to starve herself. Thankfully I did not need to concern myself, because only after a few minutes the alarming feeling passed and I was able to return to Mass. Thank You, Lord!

Using this very positive approach also brought me relief in two other fasting experiences. During one fast I felt that I was having a severe heart attack. The other occurred when I had a double nosebleed on the thirtieth day of a fast. Once again God came through for me.

If God were asking me to do these fasts for His purposes, then He had to take care of me. "You asked me Lord, now sustain me." I have used this prayer under other circumstances and it works—that is, if it is His will and not mine.

I need to add that if these situations had been reversed, and my husband were the one fasting instead of me, I would not have been able to handle these situations as well as he did. My husband Speight certainly had to have complete trust in God during these ordeals. If we all had faith the mere size of a mustard seed, we could surely move mountains.

"You Protest Too Much"

As the leader of a Charismatic prayer group in town in the early 80s, I decided since it was May 1ˢᵗ that the Blessed Mother wanted us all to have a rosary. The month of May is especially dedicated to Mary, Queen of Heaven and Earth. Most of the recipients were very pleased with the rosary gift; however, there was one lady who was not overjoyed with her present. She voiced her negative feelings to all of us. At this particular time most Charismastics were not involved with the idea of the Mother of God being an intercessor. A few of us definitely were; however, most were not. Today this has changed. At the prayer meetings I attended in Virginia we always started our gathering with the recitation of the rosary.

Seven months later, I happened to overhear a conversation before one of our meetings between the same lady protester and another member of the group. She now mentioned that she had her entire family say the rosary every evening during Advent! Even the hardhearted have a difficult time resisting the Blessed Mother's prompting!

"Thank You, Lord, for Everything"

The "Thank You" prayer along with "I Bless You, I Love You Lord," is one of the most powerful prayers I know. It is saying to God, "I trust You totally. You love me and all is well." No matter what my head may be telling me at the moment, my spirit knows that God is taking care of my every need and I thank Him. This applies to all situations. With this prayer comes extraordinary peace. God is protecting me and there is nothing to fear as a result. He has given me much practice in a variety of situations to witness the results of this simple prayer.

An incredible example of this was when I found myself in the midst of a hailstorm with silver dollar sized ice particles. It pounded the skylights in my living-room area. Inside the house the deafening noise sounded like the roar of a freight train. Although I had encountered a hailstorm near Yellowstone Park, which left the windshield of my car badly pitted, nothing compared to this storm. Since my husband was away at the time, all emergencies had to be handled by me and me alone. It was not a comforting thought that the skylights high above my head could possibly shatter at any moment. Time had come for serious prayer. All that issued forth from my mouth was, "Thank You, Thank You, Thank You, Lord," which quickly brought forth great peace. In a few minutes the hail subsided and miraculously there was no damage requiring immediate repairs to our house. Unfortunately, this was not the case locally. Many folks had their skylights damaged as well as other serious destruction to their homes and their vehicles. It was recorded that hail was falling to the ground at 100 mph. "Thank You, Lord," certainly worked for hail!

"Cobra Snakes?"

The contemplative Sisters in the compound where we lived in Calcutta, India, had adoration once a week from 10:00 – 11:00 p.m. It seemed a wonderful time for me to spend with Jesus, but as I wandered along the narrow garden paths toward the house where the Sisters resided, what often entered my mind was, "Could there be any snakes in this vegetation? Any Cobra snakes perhaps?" After several of these nightly excursions, I approached one of the Sisters with my concern about snakes being present near their house. Her reply was, "Oh, the Cobras come out every morning about 10:00 a.m. to sun themselves in the backyard. However, they are never in the front yard." Guess what? I was never in the backyard at 10:00 a.m., nor was I ever again in the front yard at 10:00 p.m.! Afterwards I asked Jesus to arouse me before 10:00 p.m. if He wished me to trek to the Sister's dwelling for adoration. Somehow I always awakened at 10:30 p.m. (Today I feel as though I would be more trusting in God.)

My fears did not just relate to the outdoor snakes. We slept in a compound that was connected to a small room, which was used for eating purposes. If bananas were left out the night before, we would often find their skins lying about on the compound floor the next morning. Likewise, if the food was not securely placed in a container, it too could possibly be missing the next morning. Located on the second floor of the building, our shower area had an open drainpipe which was used as passageway for the local rat population. My friend Lou told me that she would not get up and go to the bathroom at night unless I went first. Rats did not bother me one bit, but the mere thought of a Cobra snake did. Remembering Kipling's story of the Cobra snake that would go up the drainpipe, I would enter the bathroom in the evening with great trepidation. My prayer every night was, "Thank You, Lord, for no Cobra snakes in the bathroom!"

"It's Not Always for You"

My blood went into an old farmhouse that we reno-
vated in New Hampshire. I stained beams by candlelight
at midnight, painted floors, and worked on all sorts of proj-
ects that normally I would never have tackled. Decorating
was really my true passion. It turned out to be an incredibly charming house; therefore, when my husband decided
it was too cold for him to live there upon retiring and that
old houses did not appeal to him at this stage in his life, it
was quite painful for me to let it go. The house was for
someone else who also had a God who loved and cared
about them. It turned out to be a gift for a lady who very
obviously felt the same way about the old farm as I did. All
you have to do is drive by the front door to see how much
she treasures what God has given her.

Once again we had built another house in an inlet
off the Chesapeake Bay in Mathews, Virginia. It was a
truly wonderful home. I felt this was perhaps going to be
the place where we would stay forever. My husband's
cousin referred to our location as utopia. Unfortunately,
since we were still living at a condominium in Ocean
View, Virginia, we were spending only a few days in our
new home from time to time. The summer it was completed, we had to make a decision as to whether it was
going to be our permanent residence or not. My husband

announced it was situated too far from his favorite golf course for him to be happy with this location. It seemed that this paradise was not meant to be for us either.

When our house was nearly completed, another client of our builder was trying desperately to come up with plans for their house. They purchased a piece of property only a few houses away from ours and were in the throes of what sort of dwelling would make them happy. One day she shared her great dilemma with me, until she entered our house and exclaimed, "This is it!" Would we mind if they duplicated our home? The lady mentioned the night prior she had been praying to the Lord to help find her the right house. I must say I did hesitate for a few moments before I said it was O.K. God was certainly taking care of her, courtesy of the Drummonds and His Honor. The Lord has ways to make the whole world happy as long as we cooperate.

"Holy Land Cross"

While with my pilgrimage group in Jerusalem, I was asked with two other ladies to carry the wooden cross for several stations, including the nineth station. As we followed in Jesus' footsteps I suddenly experienced an overwhelming force pushing me to the ground. It was most difficult for me to remain standing, but I resisted falling. This happened to be the nineth station where Jesus fell for the third time; however, I could not bring myself to say, "Yes Lord, I 'truly' follow in Your foot-steps."

"Immaculate God"

While doing the Stations of the Cross at the Fatima Shrine in Portugal, I became aware of an incredible amount of trash strewn around along the paths between the various stations. It occurred to me that God wanted some action taken. I then found myself walking behind the group busily grabbing all sorts of discarded junk out of the vegetation lining our winding footpath. I quickly visualized my white skirt and light-colored blouse getting covered and stained with dirt.

What complicated matters was that my hip was giving me problems during this particular time in my life. This added to the general discomfort of having to bend continually or to simply walk the distance required to do the Stations. When God wants it, no matter how outrageous, if we consider the request and are willing to say, "Yes," we will be covered from head to toe by His Majesty. Not only did God give me the strength that day, but also, as I climbed aboard the bus, I beheld a perfectly immaculate white skirt and a spotless blouse!

"Ask and You Shall Receive, Cheaply"

The Pope, John Paul II, was to be in Louisiana in September and my daughter had managed to obtain an extra pass from her local parish for me. Unfortunately, no apparent funds were available in our household for travel at that time; consequently, my husband announced if I wished to go I had to find a super cheap airline ticket.

Two of my grandchildren were visiting us in Connecticut that August; therefore, while waiting in line at the airport to check them in for their flight, it occurred to me to ask the ticket agent if any inexpensive fares were available for Louisiana during the time of the Pope's appearance. In checking her computer the agent discovered $118 dollar round trip ticket from New York to New Orleans. There were only a few seats left!

What an amazing airfare! God sure wanted me to see Pope John Paul II; cheaply even! Ask and you shall receive!

"Have You Wiped the Slate Clean?"

My daughter went to confession after six years of not doing so. She had the priest announce to her that it was no coincidence that it happened to be Mary Magdalene's Feast Day. On the following weekend a young male came into her life that she eventually married. He is a perfect husband for our daughter.

I always ask young adult Catholics who maintain that God has not put a suitable mate in their lives as of yet, "Have you gone to confession lately? Perhaps you need to wipe the slate clean."

It is quite difficult to put new wine into an old wineskin, just ask Jesus!

"St. Michael, Help!"

The St. Michael Prayer has always been a very potent prayer for me, particularly when I have felt attacked physically at very crucial moments in my life. I have used it on several occasions. For instance, I used it when I was getting ready for an extremely important trip and all of a sudden felt very ill. It also helped when I was shopping in a grocery store and a migraine headache suddenly manifested itself, which in its initial stages can render me almost sightless. There have been times where I have gotten a migraine where I could have used it to avoid what I was supposed to do. For instance, getting one prior to attending a funeral. Likewise, prior to a luncheon engagement I suddenly had severe pain in my chest, which could have offered an excellent excuse for canceling the appointment.

I have always seen how important what followed these "monkey wrenches" were in God's plan. They were strictly deterrents to His will. By calling on St. Michael we can rid ourselves of these short circuits if they are not God's intention for us at the moment.

St. Michael's Prayer

St. Michael the Archangel defend us in Battle. Be our protection against the wickedness and snares of the Devil. May God rebuke him, we humbly pray and do Thou O Prince of the Heavenly Host by the power of God, cast into Hell Satan, and all the evil spirits, who roam through the world seeking the ruin of souls. Amen.

"Is the Pope for Everyone?"

When I saw the Pope in Louisiana years ago, it turned out to be a most eventful day. At 2:30 that morning I was busy running to the bathroom, very ill from consuming some tainted seafood earlier in the evening. We were supposed to leave the house for New Orleans, an hour away, by 3:30 a.m., in order to be able to park our car in a designated area on the outskirts of the city. The inner city streets were cordoned off for the Pope's ride in his Pope-mobile through the downtown area. He traveled along the streets before his scheduled 4:00 p.m. Mass on the University of New Orleans athletic field. God alone gave me the grace to travel that morning.

We spent the early hours of the day walking the streets of the inner city, biding our time until the Pope's appearance. Later we sat on a campstool from 1:00 p.m. until 4:00 p.m. in the middle of a huge field. I encountered sun so blazingly hot, that I knew I was being purified by fire. Then came a thunderstorm that seemed to cleanse us with "holy water." Last of all came the Pope, but not until we were all properly chastened for God's vicar. It was a most holy experience.

When leaving the field I mentioned to a priest, who was beside me, how meaningful I found this experience to be. He literally spat at me, "The Pope, Achh." My daughter happened to hear this exchange and the venom in his voice took us both aback.

In future years I have heard many remarks made by priests such as "When we rid ourselves of this Pope, there will be fresh air in the church. Who knows what the Pope says? He's over there and we are over here." Many remarks are made concerning the need for women priests and married priests. One priest, who taught spiritual direction classes, stated at a conference that the Pope is like a Pharisee. The Jews blindly followed the Pharisees and therefore missed Jesus. There are those who believe that there are Catholics blindly following the Pope who are likewise being misled. When I confronted him with his statement and asked for an explanation, I was told that there should be married priests. Could it be possible that what he truly was saying was that he himself wished to be married? If a priest has a love affair with God and the Church, there should be no need for another spouse. If he does not, it is highly unlikely that he will survive the lack of intimacy.

I feel that one must take time each day in order to establish such a personal relationship with God, be it either priest or layperson. In our present harried world, particularly with our preoccupation for social action, this is sadly neglected. We cannot feed others without first being fed ourselves. "Do goodism," is as bad as "Do badism." How are we to know if it is God's will without listening and utilizing all the aids: the Eucharist, Bible, rosary, adoration, prayer, etc. that are offered to us through the Catholic Faith?

It seems obvious to me that Pope John Paul II is not only a philosopher and a theologian, but also a lover of God and mankind. How can we disbelieve that he has a hotline to God and is doing His will? He spends much time daily in prayer with God and with the Blessed Mother as the intercessor. He is her Pope.

What God said to me years ago, when I wished to pursue a theology degree, which obviously was not what He had in mind for me at the time, was, "Nancy, I have lots of theologians but only a few lovers."

"Lost Sheep"

On our way to the Eucharistic Conference in Seoul, Korea, my friend Vera and I missed our connecting flight in Japan and consequently our hookup with the group arriving from New York. They simply left without us. What to do? Thank goodness I had done quite a bit of traveling; therefore, I was not terribly concerned. My friend was very comfortable journeying in Europe, being Czechoslovakian herself, but had not previously been in the Orient. Many airport employees spoke minimal English, but only in customs were we able to locate someone who fully understood our dilemma and could be of assistance. The airlines found us lodgings for the night, dined us royally, and sent us on our way to Seoul the next morning. Unfortunately, there was another problem. We did not have the name of the hotel in Korea where we were supposed to join our pilgrimage group. When the travel agent sent us our itinerary they did not, at that time, include a designated hotel in Seoul. If no one met us at the airport in Korea, we would be lost. Ten o'clock Japanese time I phoned the travel agent in the States for help. Fortunately for us, there was a twelve-hour time difference and we were able to reach someone who could be of assistance. They were able to provide us with the name of our hotel in Seoul and reassured us that someone would certainly be there at the airport to greet us upon our arrival.

When we arrived in Seoul, there was no one to welcome us. To make matters worse, after taking a cab to the hotel, we again found no sign of our group. Thankfully, we encountered a very gracious gentleman in the lobby who generously offered to take us to the Olympic Village where the conference was now in session. He then located seats for us in the large auditorium and assured us that he would return very shortly, after finding our absent fellow travelers. The Eucharistic Conference is a worldwide meeting of clergy and laymen. Consequently, it was not an easy task for him to locate our missing comrades. Eventually he did return and we joined a group who seemingly was very unconcerned about our whereabouts. The Father, who was head of the pilgrimage, was not used to the role of being in charge of folks traveling overseas. I'm sure he simply entrusted God with the task of finding "His Lost Sheep," which He did. Thank You, Lord!

"Are You Present Holy Spirit?"

When we are trying our utmost to know, love, and serve God, incredible things often happen to show us how much He really loves us. He truly takes care of us.

This demonstrated itself on a recent trip to Louisiana with my friend Kay, who has a healing ministry. God showed all of us how we can pick up a serpent, as St. Paul did in the Gospel, and be totally protected. This is the way God explained my ordeal to me the next morning at Mass. We were attending a large prayer meeting one night made up of thirty to forty people. After Kay spoke about God's ministry, which He had gifted her with for the last fifteen years, people were invited to step forth for personal prayers.

We all became aware that the Holy Spirits' presence was not as powerful as on prior occasions. I felt called to speak to Kay confidentially about perhaps adjourning to a bedroom for more privacy. As I turned around and headed toward the opposite end of the living room, I suddenly felt myself being propelled onto a large plate-glass coffee table nearby. The momentum of my fall totally shattered the huge piece of glass. There was a tremendous explosion and shards of glass flew everywhere. I ended up on the floor with blood dripping from one of my fingers. I also became aware of a large wet spot on the back of my blouse. I wondered if it was blood. If it was blood I knew I was seriously wounded. However, there was no sensation of pain that would indicate it was a wound. I heard Kay say, "Don't move, be quiet" and another lady hovering over me asking if I was O.K. But instead of responding to them I kept on saying, "Thank You, Lord! Thank You, Lord! Thank You, Lord!" With this prayer came incredible peace. Miraculously it was only water on my shirt and not blood. Where the water came from, I do not know. Needless to say, everyone believed in miracles that night because God clearly showed us He was present in a mighty way. Amazingly enough, with such a tremendous impact with the glass I only cut one of my fingers, which did not require stitches. After the big bang, much healing took place. God had captured our attention in a very spectacular way.

Someone told me afterwards, who happened to be close by as I pitched forward into the glass, that it appeared to her I had been pushed. I certainly did not remember tripping over anything. Thank You, Lord! But please, no repeat performances!

When I asked Father later if he had heard of my ordeal, he said it was the talk of the town. Hopefully God impressed many that night. He certainly impressed me. "You can do anything, Lord."

"The Holy Spirit Strikes Again"

During the second day of my retreat in Colorado, I expressed to the Father my desire to go to confession. He agreed to meet me at 3:00 that afternoon in a small turret room reserved for this purpose. I arrived on time. The door was open, but there was no sign of the priest; therefore, I positioned myself in the chair closest to the door. Almost immediately the Holy Spirit totally overwhelmed me. I could not move. Forty-five minutes later, no priest present as yet, I removed myself from the seat and proceeded to the church.

The next morning Father apologized for not showing up. He simply stated that he forgot and offered to hear my confession after Mass. As we both entered the small room, the priest took his usual place, which just so happened to be my seat the previous afternoon.

God clearly showed me the power of the Holy Spirit, which is given to His priests for the forgiveness of sins. Since then I have been aware of this presence, to a lesser or greater degree when I am given absolution after confession. God keeps His covenant with His people.

"My Guardian Angel Strikes Again!"

As I napped on my bed late one afternoon, I was awakened by a tremendous crash that took place beside me. A large crucifix, which once hung over my bed, was now unattached and resting on the floor nearby. My husband had purchased the copper crucifix for me on one of his trips to Spain, but the wooden cross was not impressive enough for the large corpus; therefore, I dismantled an old rattan table found at the dump and used the underneath crossbar as a substantial wooden cross. The weathered wood fit in perfectly with the rustic surroundings.

Once in a while the thought entered my mind as to what might occur if the massive crucifix ever came lose from its rawhide bindings. Thankfully, God decided to save me that day because, instead of dropping straight down, it defied gravity and moved unbelievably to the far left. My guardian angel was surely on the job at that moment. Thank You, Lord!

"No, is Not the Answer"

It was during the morning of Good Friday in Garabandal, Spain, that I was climbing the mountain where the Stations of the Cross were located along the way to the summit. Our pilgrimage group was scheduled to do this together in the afternoon; but, it seemed God was calling me to climb it alone that morning. As I climbed toward the seventh Station, I suddenly could not move either upwards or downwards on the steep incline. It was a terrifying experience, especially since I was using a cane for support. Rolling down the mountain did not seem like a great alternative! No one was nearby whom I could call upon for assistance. The angels had to be my rescuers. Who else could respond to my immediate need by quickly propelling me up the rocky terrain Good Friday morning?

When I approached the seventh Station, I wished to kneel to thank God profusely for His help. As I reached out to support myself on a small rock outcropping, a large stone broke loose and landed on my foot, causing me to tumble backwards to the ground. After lying there for a short whileI was able to get up and wind my way painfully up the mountain. An injured foot did not lessen my ability to walk for miles that day. God definitely wanted me to experience His second fall on the way to the cross that Good Friday. He was not going to take "No" for an answer.

"Crosses are for Hanging"

I was cleaning a small silver crucifix with toothpaste one morning during Lent, when I noticed that the green toothpaste was turning red. It became redder and redder, even bloody red in fact. I examined my finger, which I had been using as an applicator, but there was no visible sign of a cut or abrasion. A very thought provoking incident, indeed. This crucifix, which I wore around my neck to Mass the next day, simply slipped off its cord and vanished. Obviously, this was God's special gift for someone else that day.

Then again, my daughter Sarah gave me a beautiful, silver Mexican cross for Christmas one year. It had unusual markings on it which I had never seen before. One day a stranger remarked to me that she found the fish on my cross very interesting. For years I would say to others, "God is like a deep sea fisherman trying to reel us in, but sailfish fight for their lives when hooked. We, in turn, do not realize that being caught means the beginning of life and not the end."

Hopefully, God was trying to tell me that I was now nailed to the cross, joyfully out of love for Him and to save souls. Do not allow me to wiggle free Lord, nail those nails in harder!

"Boys Will be Boys"

I have to include this funny story Father told me about one of his experiences in the confessional. A young male was busy relating his sins to him when a tremendous rumpus occurred in the booth. He could hear a raised voice proclaiming very clearly, "Johnny, you had better tell Father the truth and nothing but the truth!" The scuffling continued until Father emerged to check on what could possibly be the problem. Out of the confessional came two young males, brothers undoubtedly. Big brother was not going to allow any discrepancies in little brother's confession that afternoon! At least in the way Father perceived it.

Hopefully, you are keeping check on us too, Lord.

"Are You Listening?"

I have learned that God speaks to us through various circumstances and many different people. Years ago, my mother informed me that I never listened to anyone. This was absolutely true. When I commented to her one day that she should have insisted that I take a certain course of action in my youth, her response to me was, "Make *you* do anything?" God also let me know when I first desired a closer relationship with Him that I never listened to anyone, so how could I possibly listen to Him? We all have to start sometime, somewhere. My husband was actually the chosen one. When I listened, all was well. Hopefully, Lord, I listen to You now, at least some of the time. This has to be a big improvement over never!

"Be Sure to Listen"

Before my trip to Medjugorje, I was chatting with my daughter Barbara, who suggested that I should take a small bag with me on the plane containing a change of clothing, etc. in case my luggage was lost. I had never done this before because I preferred to keep my baggage to a minimum; however, this time it seemed reasonable for me to listen to her suggestion. When no bag arrived for me at the airport in Yugoslavia, I was prepared, thanks to Barbara.

At the start of this trip, I was standing in the terminal in New York with some gentleman going to Frankfurt, Germany. I then remembered telling the ticket agent that this too was my destination. Unfortunately, it was not my final destination. In essence, I personally sent my bag to the wrong airport. Thank You, Lord. For once I listened, but not totally!

"Acrobatic Angel?"

It was during an Easter Sunday Mass in Connecticut that I was asking God where my gift was that day? In front of me stood an unusual looking male dressed very strangely with a derby hat on his head. When we went to communion he happened to be in front of me in line. All of a sudden, he did a pratfall on the floor. One instant he was down on his buttocks and the next second he was up! The derby hat never even left his head. It was an amazing performance, one that I had only previously seen on stage. I looked around and noticed that I was the only one who had observed this feat. There did not seem to be any reaction from the communicants surrounding me.

I stayed for prayer after Mass while my two children proceeded to the parking lot. While they were waiting for me, this strange being engaged them in conversation.

An acrobatic Angel in a derby hat, Lord? It was an unforgettable Easter gift, that's for sure.

"Immediate Action"

Here again was another example of when I refused to pay attention. I had previously discerned that on this particular Sunday afternoon I was supposed to take a friend out to lunch for his birthday. When I called him, he was dragging his feet a bit; therefore, it was easier at that moment for me to let go of the idea then to pursue the matter any further.

By the time I was able to fulfill my promise to him, it was Wednesday and all sorts of turmoil had developed. For instance, we experienced an unforeseen storm right before my arrival at the restaurant. It simply did not come together as it should have. If I had tuned out all the Sunday static and taken action, as I should have, it would have been so simple. Not easy, but simple. We make life very complicated for ourselves by refusing to listen to God's will and not acting on what is being asked of us. Now, not later, Lord. Please help us to keep our hearts tuned into the right channel for immediate action, if that is Your will.

"St. Anthony to the Rescue"

After we arrived in Calcutta, India, my friend Lou and myself were trying to find Mother Theresa's Motherhouse. However, it was not easy to locate. We assumed that everyone would know where Mother Theresa lived. To our surprise, this was not the case. We located a cab driver that thought he knew where the Missionaries of Charity resided. Unfortunately, we soon found ourselves stalled in a horrendous traffic jam. Just as our situation seemed hopeless, out of a church court-yard came a man yelling, "I'm Anthony. I'm Anthony. Can I help you?" We replied, "Oh, yes Anthony, could you tell us how to get to Mother Theresa's Motherhouse?" He told us that we were headed in the wrong direction, and then showed our cabby the right way to go.

It just so happened that Lou had a great devotion to St. Anthony. He had found several diamonds that had fallen out of her rings in the past. Likewise, He certainly sent someone that day to the two "lost" women who were looking for a "lost" Motherhouse.

"Angel on the Mountain"

There have been numerous incidents in my life where I have felt as I though I have encountered angels in human form. For instance, my daughter Carol and I were in Medjugorje during her Thanksgiving school break. When on a rainy afternoon we felt called to climb the big mountain with the large cement cross on it. The area was quite deserted because of unpleasant weather conditions, however, we felt God was asking us, despite the drizzle, to remove our shoes, navigate the slippery rocks and proceed up the rocky terrain. Water was pouring off the surrounding hillside, which was an unforeseen blessing. We simply followed the stream. We experienced pleasantly cool feet part of the time and slightly numb toes the rest of the time.

At the third Station of the Cross, a young gentleman, who obviously had come off the mountain, interrupted our prayers. Bowing to us repeatedly, he exclaimed, "Thank you! Thank you! Thank you!" He then vanished and we continued upward. My daughter commented later that I flew up the mountain that day. Greeting us at the summit was a glorious sun with a multitude of rays streaming forth. It reminded me of what occurred prior to my first trip to Medjugorje in 1985.

Back then I thought God was calling me to Yugoslavia; however, I was not sure how my husband was going to respond to this request. While I was driving to New Hampshire from Connecticut one August afternoon, I was again greeted by a dazzling sun in a brilliant blue sky with a myriad of rays streaming toward earth. Glorious was the only word to describe such a spectacle. It appeared as a sign to me that all was well. Amazingly, my husband agreed to my Medjugorje pilgrimage when I phoned him that evening.

On this special day when two solitary ladies contemplated God's beautiful gift to them, our friend, whom we previously saw, appeared barefoot and joyfully brought forth bread from his knapsack and shared it with us as Holy Communion on God's holy mountain.

Could this have been an angelic presence, Lord?

"Until Death do Us Part"

A good friend was visiting me in Virginia, who seemingly at this time had tied up all of the loose ends in her life. She certainly was in the most peaceful place that I had ever seen her. However, there was one situation that existed which she still needed to handle. She mentioned she and her estranged husband were not on speaking terms at the moment. I urged her to please make amends as soon as possible.

Our encounter took place at the end of November, and by Christmas, my 50-year-old friend was dead, killed in an airplane crash. When I approached her husband at the funeral, I asked if they had reconciled their differences with one another and he responded, "Yes." I believe God takes us at the most optimum moment in our lives. If there is a God who loves us, then this has to be true. God is love. He has no choice but to love each and every one of us.

Eugenia was a wonderfully creative lady who left our town when she and her husband got a divorce. She was very much an accomplished artist in her own country. At fifty years old she developed two aneurysms in her brain, one of which she chose to have operated on, the other she opted to ignore. Her physician had explained to her that if she did not agree to surgery on the second blood vessel immediately, it would rupture within three months. My friend, finding the first operation too horrendous, decided to forgo the second operation and head for Spain instead. A year of studying art abroad appealed to her.

While she was at her farewell cocktail party, three months later Eugenia's soul departed. She was celebrating her leave; glass in hand. Bon Voyage!

If she had written the scenario for her own demise, this would definitely have been her choice. God aims to please.

My mother-in-law had a stroke in April and ended up in the hospital for three months before her death. From the reaction to her confinement it was quite obvious that she was an extremely angry lady. Her sons, understandably, felt that God would be doing their mom a big favor by taking her as soon as possible. She was in her 80's and had led a full life. However, she told me shortly before her illness that there were some things in her life she could not let go of. When people are praying for us, watch out! God uses whatever means are available, even if it means knocking us flat and draining out the venom with a giant hypodermic needle.

Examples of the changes that took place in my mother-in-law were many. For instance, a friend showed up with a priest whom she greeted with great joy. I never warned Eva that my husband's mom had little love for the church. Again, on one of my visits I sat and said the rosary out loud by her bedside without any negative reaction from her. This was truly miraculous.

Be aware when someone is ill. God may have a plan that might be quite different from our own. God knows what He is doing. Too bad we cannot get out of the way and let Him proceed with His intentions.

"God Does Provide"

My family seems to move around a lot. Instead of playing musical chairs, we play musical houses. Miraculously, God has always come up with the money at the right moment. For instance, my mother offered us funds, which were left when my father died. It was exactly the right amount we needed for a down payment on our new home in Connecticut. Then, when my mother passed away, we again received enough money to buy an old farmhouse in New Hampshire. Once again, a cottage, which we purchased in New Hampshire, had been on the market for four years before we arrived on the scene and the owners had reduced the price so we could afford it. Finally, when we moved to Idaho, revenue became available from a house which we sold within a week of the final closing of our new home. As was the common theme, it was almost the identical amount we needed.

I truly believe if God is asking us to move for Him and His purposes, He will make it possible. Searching for the right home is not even an issue. It will be there if we wish to tune into what He wants. As my husband has reminded me, we have purchased ten homes in the past eleven years and sold eight of them. Each one of them was special in their own way and also served a very important purpose.

A wonderful example of not listening to God's will was when we moved to Connecticut from Maryland. There was a house, which I resisted like the plague. I simply refused to listen at that time in my life. It was the second place the realtor wished to show me and I said, "No." The exterior of the building turned me off totally. Having been a rental property for ten years, it did not show any care by its former tenants. There was also snow covering the ground and therefore I did not see the total landscape picture.

God finally reached me in a motel room at 4:00 in the morning. While I mulled over all the other real-estate possibilities, I had to admit that none of them made any sense except the house I disliked so much. Its most impressive feature was six bedrooms; since I was expecting our seventh child in August, it could actually be ideal. Although I was extremely reluctant and still disliked the house immensely, I called the realtor and agreed to look inside.

The next morning, a contrite me, appeared in the realtor's office and announced, "I changed my mind." He responded, "Lady, people are always buying houses they hate."

In actuality this turned out to be the perfect choice for us. Once the snow melted, there was a meadow outside the porch that I dearly loved. In addition, the surrounding property was perfect. We were also able to incorporate old barn siding and large beams into the interior, making it into a very rustic and a unique abode. It became so special to me that I never saw another home in the area that appealed to me more. God, of course, knew this all along, but I did not.

Amusingly enough, I had a son-in-law who was not favorably impressed with the old beams, barn siding, etc. in our house. He expressed this upon his first visit to our home with our daughter, Mary Lou. Frankly, he did not like it at all. Three weeks after their marriage, while we were visiting with them at their new home, we asked, "Where's Dave, Mary Lou?" Her response was, "Oh, he's out in the backyard tearing down the old wooden fence so he can line the kitchen and pantry walls with the weathered wood." Never, say "never," right Lord?

"Keys Can Crucify"

God says "Pray, be joyful and say thank you for everything." As a result, He has given me much practice in order to be patient and stay peaceful each time I have locked my keys in my car. My first memorable experience was when I locked my keys in my car and hired a cab driver to drive me to the Toyota dealership for a replacement. The exciting part was that the driver had to pay for my new key because of course my purse was locked in my car!

I found that building spiritual muscle is similar to building physical muscle, except that any place and time is fine with God. We just need to trust, trust, trust in Him.

Another such experience was when I was returning to Phoenix on my way to the East Coast. I thought it most appropriate to spend a few days at the Phoenix Diocesan Desert Retreat House in Black Canyon, Arizona, before the long trip back to Virginia. It was a wonderful spot to experience oneness with our Creator. Everyone had their own separate hermitage with an inspiring view of the desert and surrounding mountains. I had witnessed coyotes chasing rabbits, eagles soaring for hours on the desert thermals, as well as quail running amongst the desert flora. One of my most thrilling moments was when a raven flew past my hermitage. He was cawing to get my attention, then proceeded to fly upside down, right side up, over and over again. What a memorable performance that was!

This particular August day I drove up the mountain to the entrance and then proceeded to get out of my vehicle to open the gate. Upon returning to my truck I discovered it was locked! Unbelievably, the engine was running and the air conditioner was on. To make matters worse, my cane as well as my pocketbook sat on the front seat. I needed to remember to stay cool, pray, and say *thank you, and make my way swiftly, like a gazelle, down the mountain*, to a campground office located on the road about half a mile away.

The man who was in attendance mentioned he normally would not have been there but the regular employee was in labor at the hospital. It took him 45 minutes to locate someone who could come open my truck. When they arrived they told me that they would open the truck and return it to me on their way back down the mountain.

In the meantime, the campground manager remarked that he had never seen these gentlemen before. Of course this made me a little apprehensive. All my personal stuff including my pocketbook was in that car. This was a very small community where everyone more-or-less knew everyone else, so I felt it was time for me to "lope" my way back up the mountain, courtesy of God. As it worked out they did not have the car open when I arrived but were successful in their attempt shortly afterwards. They were even willing to hold open the gate for me as I drove through.

It was a very special retreat—the Passion to the Resurrection. One will never get to the Resurrection without first going through the Crucifixion.

"Anything is Possible With God: The Rosary"

For years I collected all sorts of beads; be it either old beads, new beads, or in-between beads. I acquired most of them in junk shops, tag sales, or on overseas pilgrimages. I would take these necklaces apart and recycle the beads into rosaries. It was amazing to witness how some on the most unattractive pieces of plastic, wood, glass, and metal could be rearranged into such lovely rosary creations. What occurred to me while making the rosaries was, if we could say, "Yes Lord, I give You permission to pull me apart, applying some heat and pressure in the process," then in rearranging us He could produce the same astonishing results as I had witnessed in the transformation of those ugly undesirable beads.

My Rosary creations have ended up all around the world. My husband made the wooden crosses; therefore, I feel he is the recipient of much prayer worldwide.

I believe that God throws us a bone periodically to let us know that what we are doing has value. For instance, my husband and I had made rosaries for an Emmaus weekend in town for high school kids. While we sat at Mass on a Monday morning, Father told us that there was a lecture on the Blessed Mother at the Sisters of

Notre Dame Motherhouse in town after the service. The topic to be discussed was Mary, the Mother of God. Even though I was very exhausted from an intensely spiritual weekend with the kids, I felt God was asking me to attend. While there, one of the ladies in the audience spoke up announcing her daughter had attended a retreat over the weekend. She had brought home a Rosary and then had the whole family saying the prayer by that evening after dinner. God is good to let us know that it is not all for naught. He certainly made my weekend. I questioned her later to see if her child was one of those participating in our retreat and she said, "Yes."

"Thank You, Lord"

$\mathcal{A}s$ the taxi pulled up outside our house in Virginia, we became aware that my husband's red car was nowhere in sight. They had been working on the roads in the area; therefore, the taxi driver suggested that the paving company might have had the police remove it. Upon phoning the police that evening, my husband was informed that they had no record of any such vehicle. My response to all of this was "Thank You, Lord." It was amazing that neither my husband nor I were very upset at the time. That particular day we were traveling from Idaho to Virginia and were exhausted, but when my friend Kay called that evening for me to come for a visit, it seemed like the right thing to do. Amazingly enough my fatigue dissipated enough for me to drive 35 minutes to her house, spend three hours with her, and then drive home again. It was a long evening. It did not even occur to me to announce that my husband's car was missing until halfway through our conversation that night. She mentioned before I left that she felt we would somehow locate it.

As I drove home it occurred to me to look for our missing vehicle. I decided to first check in a cul-de-sac, which was well hidden from our house. Surprisingly enough, under a large tree, hidden from view, was our red car! It had obviously been towed to this location, since the vehicle was locked; however, no one in the neighborhood had been informed of any such action. They all simply said that the vehicle just disappeared one day. "Thank You, Lord."

"The Rosary to the Rescue"

The Rosary has always played a dominant role in my life. My conversion to Catholicism took place in my mid-teens around the time that my mother, who was not a practicing Catholic for many years, decided to return to her faith. My dad was an Episcopalian; hence, I was baptized and raised as such. When my brother, who was engaged to a Catholic girl, went for instruction in order to enter the church, I decided to join him. Several of my good friends were Catholic; therefore, I had developed a strong interest in the religion. The Blessed Mother was waiting for me. She introduced her child to Our Lady of Fatima and had a faithful Rosary fan almost immediately. I know that praying the Rosary kept me from falling into the pit throughout my teens and early adult years. Tempting fate with the crazy belief that I could be in total control of all situations, makes me cringe today at my naiveté. My poor guardian angel definitely worked overtime.

"Be Careful What You Say, God is Never out to Lunch"

One day while talking on the phone, I made the remark to a friend that, "God was a pain in the you know what." She was horrified. There was deep silence on the other end of the line. We then continued our conversation, and after my explanation for this perception, she seemed to feel a bit more comfortable with what I had said. Later she remarked that as she walked away from the phone, she happened to glance at the picture of Jesus hanging on her wall and he was laughing.

Weeks later on a pilgrimage to Medjugorje, God showed me in no uncertain terms just how much of a pain He was. It was Easter week, so from Wednesday until the following Tuesday evening I was not able to go to the bathroom. Talk about crucifixion, this was it! What unbelievable pain! God is creative and I certainly had chosen His weapon by saying that He was a pain in the you-know-what!

Years ago when my husband was in the service, we lived across the street from a man who was constantly having trouble with the water pipes in his house. Interestingly enough, he himself developed bladder cancer. So after he was discussing his illness, I blurted out, "You always did have a problem with your plumbing." Boy, did I pay a price for that one. My bladder has given me a fit for years!

Some ladies were gathered for lunch at my house. One of the members of the group, whose husband was a politician, mentioned that the reason his skin was flushed was because he suffered from skin cancer. From out of nowhere, came the remark, "Gee, that is the first thin-skinned politician I ever heard of." Silence reigned. This lady is now deceased, a cancer victim herself. I too became a skin cancer victim!

We need to watch our mouths, folks. We may have to eat those words, courtesy of God.

"Dogs Can be Helpful"

Art Buckwald was having a happening one evening in a vacant movie theater in the northwest section of Washington, DC. My friend Lou, her daughter Lisa, and I, with my German shepherd dog named Winnie, took off in a Volkswagen bug for a big night in town. No way was I willing to walk those dark streets in that section of the city without some added protection. Therefore, I had to bring Winnie with us. When we approached the old movie house, it occurred to me to ask the policeman who was directing traffic by the front entrance if he would be willing to hold Winnie during the performance, but he declined. Too bad, he would have made a very impressive cop with his German shepherd companion. Fortunately, the ticket lady allowed me to bring Winnie into the building with us.

Buckwald gave a stimulating performance. His talk about Sister Clarita's work (Serigraphs), which was the main reason we were all present, was delightfully humorous. At the close of the program the audience ended up sharing bread that was broken and passed amongst us. It was definitely a joyful happening. Winnie, our dog, was wonderful. She never reacted negatively to her surroundings. However, I could just imagine how perplexing it was for those people who came up the dark aisle and discovered a furry body in the process. The laughter, the clapping, and people stumbling over her body, never disturbed this peaceful animal.

Our prayers, plus Winnie, decidedly provided us with a fun filled evening.

"*Everything Has a Purpose*"

It was during a drive down a highway that my mind momentarily drifted off into oblivion. I had missed my turnoff for the New Jersey Turnpike. All of a sudden I was in unfamiliar territory. It was an extremely deserted area. Thankfully, I quickly located a service station and asked for instructions on how to get back to the thruway. The directions seemed simple enough, but there was a problem. When I looked for the stoplight where I was supposed to turn, it was nonexistent. It became clear that I better seek more explicit directions.

There were several stores in the area so I chose one, parked, and entered the establishment. It appeared to be deserted; however, back behind some display cases were a man, a woman, and a young girl, who happened to be clutching a shocking pink dress to her bosom. Startled at my appearance, they stood there wide-eyed as I approached. Silence reigned. Finally I was able to open my mouth to ask if I was on the right street to the turnpike. The man informed me that I was. The stoplight was simply far enough away that I could not see it from such a distance. When I left the shop, all I could think of was the young girl. She had grabbed her dress to cover her nudity when she became aware of my presence. There was a strange contraption on the floor nearby, which looked as though it may have been a vacuum cleaner. Who knows what it really was.

Needless to say, my mind never wandered during the rest of my trip South. I felt called to do a lot of praying for those folks back off the turnpike. God gets our attention to pray for others under some pretty strange circumstances!

"A Hitler in All of Us"

I had just returned to the States from Poland and was attending a small dinner party given by a friend. One of the places our pilgrimage group chose to visit was Auschwitz. What God impressed upon my soul during this ordeal was that there was a Hitler in all of us. Given the right circumstances with someone pushing the right button, we, in our fallen nature, have the capacity for destruction.

I mentioned this fact to a couple with whom I was speaking. It evoked two very different responses. The husband acknowledged that there was this element present within him, while his wife refused to believe any such tendency existed in her.

At the dinner table, a very animated discussion ensued concerning drugs. The lady, who had so passionately denied having any Hitler in her, came forth vehemently with, "I would kill every drug dealer!" I asked her if she remembered saying, "There's no Hitler in me!" No response was forthcoming.

While on a trip to Israel, I visited the Holocaust Museum in Jerusalem. It was an unforgettable experience, which touched the depths of my being. My soul wept. Never having experienced anything like this before, I realized that the inner pain and sadness, which I felt was so deep, had nothing to do with my head. My weeping was within—no tears were visible.

"Take it Where You Can Get It"

On a pilgrimage to the LaSalette Shrine in the French Pyrenees Mountains, we were traveling by bus late one night on roads filled with numerous hairpin turns and treacherous drop-offs. By the erratic way in which our driver was navigating this mountainous road, we realized that he needed God's help. We had visited various sites of interest during the day and stopped for dinner. Obviously, after so many hours of difficult driving, he was tired—on the verge of falling asleep.

Most of the passengers were dozing at this hour. However, there were a few of us in the back of the bus who became aware of the driver's urgent need for prayers. A few feet of movement one way or another on this narrow road could have meant death for all of us. Passionately, we recited the Rosary.

What was interesting was that the bus driver previously had a discussion with us concerning religion. He clearly stated that he did not accept any of our beliefs.

As we departed from the bus after our harrowing ride, I knew that I had to offer him a rosary, which I had made and brought with me to present to someone in need on the trip. He eagerly accepted the gift saying that he was going to keep it on the bus in the glove compartment. More than likely he was able to see us intensely saying the Rosary for him in the back of the bus through his rearview mirror. He knew he had a desperate need for prayer that night, Catholic or non-Catholic. Take it where you can get it, right Lord?

"The Lord Giveth and The Lord Taketh Away"

I was attending the Eucharistic Conference in Seoul. We had just finished a spaghetti lunch, Korean style, and were told by our leader that we were to attend a dinner that night sponsored by various Catholic families in the diocese. My roommate and I were assigned to the same family; consequently, we were transported by our host directly from the conference center to their home immediately following the conclusion of the activities. To celebrate the special event, all the ladies were beautifully attired in traditional Korean dress. Unfortunately, I have never eaten anything containing tomato sauce that did not end up displayed on the front of my apparel for the whole world to see! Lunch that day was no exception! We were not returning to our hotel rooms until after the night's festivities; therefore, changing my blouse was not an option. The only solution was for me to readjust my large nametag to a lengthwise position in order to hide the unsightly red spot. It looked a bit strange, to say the least; however, fortunately for us, only one member of the family spoke English, so most of them were unaware of the topsy-turvy lettering on the nametag. Their son, a gentleman from Los Angeles, was our interpreter for the evening. The universal language of the night was *thank-you's* and laughter. My friend Vera, myself, as well as the non-English speaking members of the family, laughed our way joyfully through the festivities.

It was a wonderful experience, despite the fact that because of my bad hip we were not able to enjoy the meal Korean style, seated on cushions around a low table. Instead, Vera and I dined at a breakfast bar in the kitchen. Nevertheless, this did not dampen our host's enthusiasm for one moment. All of a sudden it occurred to us that we did not come bearing gifts. Some very quick thinking was necessary on our part. We decided that Vera's Czechoslovakian crystal rosary and my silver rosary ring from Fatima, as well as a wooden cedar cross from around my neck, which my husband had made, would be our gifts. They were delighted with these very personal presents. God does rise to the occasion.

After we left Korea, we went to Hong Kong for a short visit before proceeding to Mainland China. While there, I asked the Lord what kind of cross should I substitute for the one left in Korea. He suggested a large ivory colored crucifix, which I carried in my pocket. It was an exact replica of the black crosses worn by many nuns. There was one problem. I had no chain or cord to attach it to except the green string from my green scapular. When I approached Father with this very obvious cross, he informed me that if I insisted on wearing it, we all might end up in jail! Our kind Chinese guide who joined us later, said that it was perfectly all right for me to be seen adorned with a crucifix. As a result, strange things happened when the population observed this Christian symbol. I had natives surreptitiously make the sign of the cross in my presence numerous times. Soldiers however, were not pleased and looked away. One lady pulled her own cross out of her blouse and gleefully pointed to mine and to her own. This was the year of the Tiananmen Square episode and there was still marshal law in Beijing. Soldiers with machine guns patrolled the square as well as other areas of the city.

We then visited a Catholic church, a former candy factory, which had only been open for two years. I felt called to pass out wooden rosaries, purchased in Seoul originally, to a few of the priests as well as several parishioners. Although I purchased these rosaries and had them blessed that morning to bring back to the States, I felt God had other intentions for them. I knew instinctively it was necessary to be very cautious in dispensing the rosary beads, not allowing the general public to observe. They were all received joyfully. As I boarded the bus for our return trip, I knew God likewise wanted my ivory crucifix to remain in China. I dashed back to the church and gave it to a very holy priest, who was delighted with his gift. This particular crucifix, I discovered back in Hong Kong, glowed in the dark. Who knows whether these simple priests in a small Chinese town had ever before encountered florescent objects? God could make an impression! I read in a Catholic newspaper nine months later that the government had thrown two priests from this area into jail for being Roman Catholics. It is food for thought, that's for sure.

Once again, after giving away my ivory crucifix I was without one. However, Jesus soon helped me locate some gold enameled crucifixes in a Beijing flea market tucked in amongst a multitude of other items. The Lord giveth and the Lord taketh away!

"Angels Passing By"

One day I was in a grocery store where the clerk at the checkout counter offered his assistance. I declined, thinking that with only three bags of food I did not need his help. However, this turned out not to be the case. Since I use a cane, the items proved to be too heavy for me to manage with one hand, therefore, the shopping cart was needed after all. While I placed the last bag in the back of my truck, I suddenly became aware that the shopping cart was barreling down a steep driveway heading for the middle of a busy city street. With no curb in sight and 4:00 traffic in progress, this scene was terrifying!

Miraculously, the insane movement stopped just at the edge of the highway. Unfortunately, it then proceeded to turn perpendicular to the thoroughfare picking up momentum as it accelerated down another sharp incline and headed toward a red-parked car. The red vehicle made quite an impression on me, as I envisioned the runaway cart making quite an impression on it! As these thoughts raced through my mind, a young male out of nowhere sped past me and grabbed the wayward cart just seconds before a collision. I did not see anyone in the parking lot until his sudden speedy appearance. Could it be another angel Lord?

This is one more incident where I refused to listen. If I had accepted the clerks offer for help, a near tragedy would never have occurred. Please teach us to listen, Lord!

"Are We Put to the Test?"

Our pilgrimage was on its way from Spain to France when we were stopped at the border and were told that we could not enter the country. In checking our passports, they discovered we had two Polish citizens on board as well as three Philippine ladies. This could be a disaster as far as our trip was concerned. It was time to pull out our rosaries and ask for the Blessed Mother's prayers. How could she resist? We were on our way to Our Lady's Shrine in Lourdes.

An hour and a half later, after numerous rosaries, the guards at the border agreed to let us enter. However, they said that they would allow admittance only if our bus driver was willing to relinquish his passport, and they promised to return it when we departed the country. Obviously, it was God's plan that we complete our pilgrimage, but not without putting us to the "test" along the way.

"Have Car, Will Travel"

One Thursday morning, while praying in Idaho, I realized that God wanted me to leave for Arizona the next morning. This could be complicated because my daughter, Carol, was expected to leave Louisiana that Friday to visit us in Idaho and it was going to take me two days to get to Scottsdale. It did not make sense to leave then while my family was coming to visit. However, my husband, Speight, agreed that it was necessary for me to drive by myself to Scottsdale in order to obtain an appointment with a doctor at the Mayo Clinic concerning my hip.

Interestingly enough, that Friday morning we received a phone call from Carol saying that she had lost the transmission in her car and it was going to be days before the garage would be able to replace it.

As it worked out, all according to God's schedule and not mine, I left Friday morning without a doctor's appointment in Arizona, prayed over names in the phone book on Monday, found a physician who could see me on Wednesday morning, and by Friday evening had returned to Idaho. My daughter then arrived on Sunday.

Maybe I should include that I was, at the time, a near seventy-year-old woman who used a cane because of a bad arthritic hip and a herniated disc in my back. It is only through God's grace that I am able to drive for hours at a time without stopping—if it is His will, that is, and not mine. A year ago I also drove fourteen hours from Birmingham, Alabama, to Norfolk, Virginia, nonstop except for an occasional pit stop. The impossible is possible with the Almighty, if we are willing to die to self-will and say, "Yes Lord," to His will.

"Prayers Answered"

God has always provided funds for us when we have had a great need in our life. It seems quite amazing that we were able to put seven kids through college. In fact, during one period of time, we had four children in college simultaneously, each in a different school and in a different area.

We were working on an old farmhouse in New Hampshire one summer. There was no septic system and not any money available to construct one. A thousand dollars was desperately needed in order for us to have a place for our daughter and her little ones to stay during their visit from Louisiana. I prayed, "God, do something if this is what You want!" Our son Dick was in our truck waiting to pull out onto the main road near our home in Connecticut, when his friend came zipping around the corner in his car, plowing into the side of our vehicle in the process. What do you know? The insurance company paid us a thousand dollars that week, enough for the septic system. We all had a great vacation. Just never try to second guess God as to how He hopes to accomplish what you are asking for, if it is His will, that is.

I felt that God was asking me to go to Medjugorje for a month in October, but my husband informed me that he did not have the funds for such a trip. "Don't plan on it," he said. I had gotten pretty good about saying to the Lord, "If You want it, then You take care of it." As long as I had no great feeling one way or another concerning His decision, He came forth in a most interesting fashion. The key for me is to say, "I really don't care," and mean it.

We had just made a final settlement on a house we were buying in New Hampshire when the people who had been renting it previously came forth with three months back rent. My husband now announced that I had money for Yugoslavia, just a day before the deadline to sign up for the pilgrimage. God does provide.

"Black Cats Can be Hazardous"

I realized that I had no alternative but to get into my car after I attended Mass in Rexburg, Idaho and head for Arizona. However, I emerged from the service realizing that I had locked my keys in my car! The journey started out to be one of those "big trust" trips! My good friend Elaine offered to take me to the golf course in Ashton, Idaho, where hopefully I could locate my husband, Speight. When we arrived at the County Course, Speight greeted us on the greens near the road. It was a miracle of miracles. God loves us, even if we are disconnected half the time. Naturally this made my departure from Idaho much later than expected.

Once I got on the highway I headed towards Idaho Falls. Almost immediately a black cat appeared out of nowhere several feet in front of my car. I thought it would be impossible to avoid running it over. After my vehicle passed over him, I looked back in my rearview mirror to see if his body was visible on the road. Thankfully, I noticed him sitting upright on the grassy median strip. Cats are known to have a number of lives!
This one definitely had more than one!

At this point I started to pray nonstop. I asked God whether this trip was necessary and if it was His will to do so. How simple it would have been to turn around and go home, but my discernment said, "No," continue onward.

I always felt that pilgrimages or journeys, which start out being difficult, were especially graced, and this visit to Arizona certainly was. "Just keep me in gear, Lord, but please no more black cats!"

"Anyone, Anywhere"

The two of us were chatting while we worked on the Catholic School book drive one fall. My new friend had recently moved to our town from Ohio; therefore, we did not know each other except in a casual way. She shared her interest in the Charismatic prayer meetings, which took place at the Cathedral in Bridgeport, and then invited me to attend one with her. As I mentioned before, "Charismatic" was not my favorite word. I associated it with Holy Rollers. However, at this time I was desperately looking for a deeper personal relationship with God. Daily masses, the rosary, reading the Bible, just were not bringing me the results I desired. When the last of our first five children left for college, I knew I had to pursue God wholeheartedly, no more straddling the fence. The fact that I dealt with five teenagers in the late 60s left me reeling, to say the least.

My new acquaintance mentioned a strange incident to me, which had occurred while she was in the confessional. The priest announced that Nancy Drummond was looking for something also. She did not have the faintest idea who Nancy Drummond was and neither of us had ever encountered a Father who revealed anyone's name during confession. In the spring I had approached Father with some questions concerning my religion, which I found perplexing, and he frankly stated that he did not know the answers. God obviously wanted me to follow the path I had rejected in the past and one that later proved to be such an important piece of the puzzle in my spiritual life. "Who asked you anyway?" is God's bottom line.

He can use anyone, anywhere.

"God of the Byways"

I was traveling north on I-91, from Connecticut to New Hampshire, when I had an experience, which clearly showed me that God was taking total care of me. It was 3:30 p.m. on a Friday and traffic was heavy but moving at a good pace. After fighting with drowsiness for several hours, I finally succumbed. I was in the right lane traveling about 65 miles an hour when I fell asleep momentarily. When I awakened, I discovered my car had crossed over into the left lane and was now plunging down a steep ravine. All that I was aware of was the word, "Jesus" coming forth from my mouth. Before this incident occurred, I had been saying the Rosary. Now God was obviously taking over, since my mind was totally out of gear. I was only able to repeat His name and hold on to the steering wheel for dear life.

Miracle of miracles, I did not hit the brakes. Instead, I held the wheel without attempting to steer in a terrain, which was impossible to navigate. The car headed for a steel post at the bottom of the steep incline. Miraculously, it went right around the steel post. A large metal grate loomed on the horizon and the car skirted around it as well. God's retinues of angels were working overtime. I was out of control and God was in control! Eventually, the terrain evened out and the truck came to a complete stop all by itself. Amazingly, I was then able to put it in gear and continue on my way to New Hampshire.

The first thing I felt compelled to do once I exited the highway was to call my daughter Mary Lou, for whom I had been baby-sitting. I told her that I nearly got killed on the I-91. She had warned me before I left that I should leave Connecticut as early as possible, for the traffic would be horrendous on a Friday afternoon. Normally during a long trip, I would have stopped for gum or a diet coke to keep me from getting drowsy. The decision to do otherwise was obviously not a wise one.

Afterwards, I spoke to my daughter Carol in Louisiana. She informed me that her High School religion class was saying the Rosary for their parents and family just about the time I had my near death experience. God is good!

God speaks to us if we would only listen. Three weeks before this traumatic incident, my husband had suggested that we trade my truck in because it had 115,000 miles on it. I stubbornly refused. There was an inordinate attachment on my part to my vehicle. It was in great shape until I hit the lumps and bumps in the ravine and started to fall apart almost immediately after the incident. If I had paid attention to my husband's request, maybe this episode would have never taken place. One thing I have learned from that experience is, whenever my husband says that it is time for us to get rid of a car, I agree, whether I want to or not!

"Be Careful What You Pray For"

My friend Sarah and I, when we were two eighteen year olds, sat in a canoe in the middle of the river praying for some excitement in our lives. All of our friends had vanished this particular Saturday and we were bored. That evening we rowed across the creek to a clubhouse in the neighboring summer community. Because we found nothing of interest, we decided to wander out on the highway and head for the roadhouse, about a half mile away.

We walked as quickly as possible along this dark wooded and sparsely traveled road. Suddenly, a car filled with drunken males approached us. They were obviously seeking some excitement of their own. As they drove out of sight momentarily, Sarah and I discovered a billboard, which we quickly climbed behind, and then prayed like crazy that we would not be seen. When they returned, thankfully, they could not find us. When they banished from our view, we ran like crazy for the roadhouse and sat inside trying to catch our breath. Unfortunately, to our dismay, our obnoxious pursuers found us. Tears were streaming down Sarah's face as both of us refused to enter into any sort of conversation with these repulsive characters. After what seemed like an eternity, they left. It was then midnight and we were far away from our rowboat.

We decided to head back down the dark highway as quickly as possible, but just as we neared the billboard, once again, our assailants returned. Thank God for billboards because that particular advertisement in the middle of nowhere saved our lives. Previously, when we left the roadhouse, we remembered that the barbershop next door was still open for business. In the past I remembered that one of my friends had mentioned what a nice guy the owner of the establishment was. Having no other alternative, we ran back to the barbershop and sat on the steps for a short while until we found the courage to approach the owner with a plea for help. After he closed shop for the evening, he generously gave us a ride to where our boat was docked.

Thank You, Lord. It took many years before I had the craziness to ask God to give me another adventure!

It was during a visit with my brother and sister-in-law in Annapolis that I suggested to Anita that we should go off together for an adventurous morning. Give us some excitement, Lord!

Well, we asked and He gave us excitement! We were driving down a very narrow winding country road after leaving her son's newly constructed home. We suddenly encountered a small "high-rise" truck, which appeared out of nowhere. It whizzed around a corner and then was literally on top of us. In order to avoid a collision, he had driven up on the bank of the road, but was now in the process of toppling down onto our car. Anita's vehicle was only a month old. She had recently had an accident involving another truck whereby her car had been totaled. Still in the process of adjusting to the new vehicle's buttons and levers, she was desperately trying to locate reverse as the truck proceeded to lean over, almost touching our hood. It actually up righted itself and repeated this process at least three times. There was some comic relief as Anita desperately tried to find reverse and instead turned her lights and windshield wipers on and off etc. Eventually she found it. Thank You, Lord. God saved us from a really "thrilling" adventure, despite my stupid request.

The next day, I had still not learned to be more discerning and cautious with God. My brother joined us for "fun and games" on Sunday, which proved to be another eventful time. As we were leaving a service station, he started to drive down a steep incline, which led to a very busy highway. As his foot momentarily slipped off the brake pedal, we rolled out into it. Thankfully, no one was coming.

Be careful what you ask for. God is never out to lunch. He is always listening!

"Be Sure You are Listening"

It was during Lent on Good Friday that my family chose to travel from Connecticut to Annapolis, Maryland for an Easter visit with my parents. The Jersey Turnpike was awash with holiday traffic. I had volunteered to drive the first leg of our journey since my husband, a corporate pilot, had returned home late from a trip the night before.

At 10:00 in the morning, traveling Southbound, we suddenly experienced a blowout in the right front tire. Fortunately, we were only traveling between 55 and 60 miles per hour. When I attempted to decrease my speed, the left front tire also went flat. Time seemed to slow down. It was almost as if I were an observer instead of a participant. The driver in back of me was frantically trying not to run into us as the car veered from one side of the highway to the other. Suddenly, the unimaginable happened. A third tire in the rear also blew. During this ordeal, our kids in the back seat had wedged our youngest, a two year old, in-between themselves to prevent her from being tossed about in this wildly careening vehicle.

Although our car was headed for the median strip, it miraculously turned around coming to rest on the guardrail facing the opposite direction. Disbelief was written all over the faces of folks who slowly passed by. Having witnessed this incredible near accident, they could not believe there were no injuries, nor bodies strewn about on the highway. Shortly thereafter, a cop appeared who stopped all traffic and God allowed us to drive a totally dysfunctional vehicle over to the grassy side of the road where we awaited the arrival of the service truck.

Before this incident took place, my last words spoken, maybe 20 minutes prior, were, "This is Good Friday. Think about it." Needless to say, we all had plenty of time; hours even, to think about Good Friday that particular day.

Ironically enough, my car was serviced right before our trip. The mechanic had assured me the vehicle was in good shape, including the tires. Somewhere, somehow, we had picked up a nail causing the first blowout. Who knows about the others? Although it was explained to us by the traffic cop that two flat tires were not unusual, he had never witnessed three.

When we returned to Connecticut on Monday I called my oldest daughter, Carol. She was a student at the University of Maine and was not able to come home for Easter. Before I had the opportunity to tell her about our adventure, she questioned me about what happened to us on Good Friday morning. She explained that she had a terrible feeling of impending doom for the family that morning; so much so, that she felt compelled to go to church and pray for us. Carol at this period in her life was not a frequent churchgoer. Even her friend Claudette could not understand why she would go to church the morning of Good Friday when everyone attended services in the afternoon. Fortunately for us, Carol was not dissuaded from God's mission for her that morning.

Be sure your short wave is tuned to God continuously, 24 hours a day; so, when the SOS goes out for help, you can respond. You may save a life and it may even be your own. Fortunately for us, through Carol's obedience, God heard and answered her prayer. Miracles do happen through prayer.

When we feel nudged by God, and/or our guardian angel, to respond to someone's desperate situation, we must act immediately and not allow our heads to prevent us from taking action.

"Passion in Calcutta"

While I was in Calcutta, India, Sister had a woman who came to her every few days to have the bandage on her head changed. This poor soul had worked in a factory where her long hair had become entangled in the machinery, causing her to be scalped. It was tragic indeed; since, an infection had set in, which did not respond to medications and had eaten away the skin and bone exposing her brain. When Sister approached me one day and asked if I would like to watch her treat her patient, I knew I had to say "yes." As the bandage was removed, the entire inside of the ladies head became exposed. The only way I could possibly handle such a horrendous sight, which looked as though maggots were devouring half of her brain, was to see Jesus crucified in this helpless Indian lady. Twice I felt called to watch the procedure, experiencing each time, in a much deeper way, Our Lord's Passion. Sister told me later that this poor suffering soul was also three months pregnant.

"Are You Listening Mom and Dad?"

Our 17-year-old son, Richard, after attending a spirit-filled Emmaus weekend, proclaimed to our family that
he was not going to college in the fall. He felt that he
should take a year off. He was quite an accomplished
lacrosse player and had numerous college coaches con-
tacting him to see if they could interest him in attending
their school. He rejected them all. During the spring, the
high school kids and their parents were all anxiously
awaiting their acceptance slips from college. Many of the
parents asked each other who was going where? Did
your child get accepted? Where did he apply? Dick was
always a good student; therefore, it was not easy for me
to reply, "Nowhere! He had not applied anywhere." The
response was such an eye opener.

Practicing humility for me at this time was becoming an everyday occurrence. His guidance counselor was
also shocked. He could not believe that Dick, with all his
talent, was not interested in a good engineering college.
For once in my life I kept my mouth shut and just prayed
about the situation. This was not easy for me to do.

It was toward the end of March when my husband
came home from Westchester Airport where he was
based and announced that a friend of his suggested
maybe Dick would like a small college in Rhode Island.

This individual's son was attending the school and seemed very pleased with their architectural design courses. Dick had become interested in redoing old houses after we bought a 1776 farmhouse in New Hampshire. He was involved with some friends in the gutting and restoration of the structure. He soon became fascinated with working on old buildings. Dick greeted his Dad's suggestion of a visit to the college with enthusiasm. When he returned, he joyfully exclaimed that he had found his niche. As a result, neither the high school counselor nor I were happy with this particular choice. This was just another opportunity to practice keeping my mouth shut. I could only do so, however, with God's help. I told the counselor that if Dick was happy with his decision, I had to accept it as well.

Surprisingly, this particular college did not have a lacrosse team, only a lacrosse club which participated in inter-club activities. Dick was captain for several years, loving the fact that the only pressure experienced was that which he applied to himself, not by a coach with a mission. Then, by his junior year the club turned into a division III team. In his senior year he was chosen as one of the members of the Northeastern All American Lacrosse team, a great honor for him. This would most likely not have been possible if he had been a little fish in a big pond, instead of a big fish in a little pond.

In addition, Dick majored in historical preservation in college and loved it. The hands-on experience in the restoration of our old farmhouse seemed to encourage this passion.

The most important piece of the puzzle, however, was that he met Lisa there in his freshman year, who is now a doctor and his wife. She is an incredibly wonderful woman.

Afterwards, I gave a talk at an Emmaus weekend for high school students where I felt called to stress that God has a plan for each of us. It may not be our plan. This was a March retreat, so the seniors were all anxiously awaiting their acceptance slips from various colleges. Many of them were not going to get their first choices. I told them all to relax, because if my son Dick made out just great, so could they. I had to keep my mouth shut and my pride on the back burner. They and their folks may have to do the same. As a result of this, Dick has a successful construction business these days, a great wife, and two beautiful children. All courtesy of Roger William's University and God! It was definitely not "my" first choice.

"Thank You Prayer"

I happened to be in a religious bookstore Friday before Labor Day and overheard two Navy Priests talking. They were discussing Solanias Casey, a priest whom the church was trying to beatify. He was a very simple holy man who, towards the end of his life, felt that the most important thing he could tell people, those who came to him in confession or sought his advice in any way, was to thank the Lord for everything. In relating this to the two Fathers, one of the priests proceeded to say he might find it a bit difficult to do while being shelled aboard his ship at sea. The other simply thanked me.

God always makes me put my money where my mouth is. One example of this occurred on Labor Day morning at 1:30. I awakened with a horrendous pain in my chest. Initially it seemed a good idea to get out of bed without disturbing my husband. I walked up and down the hall but the pain intensified and I became panic stricken. My breathing was labored and my body was covered in a thin layer of perspiration. I felt that I might die, because at that very moment I felt like I was having a heart attack. I debated if I should wake my husband in order for him to drive me to the emergency room. Instead, what entered my mind was to say, "Thank You, Lord." I repeated it over and over again. Almost immediately, the sweating subsided and my breathing became normal. Unfortunately, however, the pain in my chest remained. Then suddenly, the phone rang.

I could not imagine who would be calling us at this hour of the morning. Was there an emergency with one of our seven kids? I answered the phone with great trepidation. The voice on the other end of the line told me it was Sarah, our youngest daughter, a nurse, who lived in Arizona. She said, "Mom, I just saw a TV news broadcast announcing that a horrible accident had taken place on the Chesapeake Bay Bridge tunnel (which was located only a few miles from where we lived) and I felt that I had to call and make sure you were OK." I told her about my awful pain, whereupon she asked me several medical questions to ascertain if it could be serious. As a result of my answers she concluded that I was probably having a bad case of indigestion. It made sense actually. I had had a very seasoned shrimp meal only hours before. She instructed me to take an antacid and to sit up tall in my chair. I did as I was told and the pain vanished immediately!

Sarah was the only human being I knew that God could have had call me at such an hour. At least certainly the only one who was a nurse taking a course on cardiac EKGs at the time! Thank You, Lord!

"Forgive and Be Forgiven"

I believe that one of the biggest hang-ups we have with God is forgiveness. "Forgive and be forgiven," says the Lord's Prayer. Forgiving oneself can be extremely difficult when we hold things against ourselves. Sometimes we often burden ourselves for many years.

Some years ago when I was in college, I was awakened one night by some of my roommates' loud voices. They had gathered in the room next to mine and were literally crucifying one of our contemporaries. It was like a shark feeding frenzy as they hurled accusations at this poor cornered creature. This gal had only been an imitation of another individual who did the exact same things that she did, only she did it with "class."

I wrestled with myself the entire time the arguing was going on. Although I wanted to muster up the nerve to go and stop the bloodshed, I did not. I was raised in a family where I was not exposed to any form of arguing. As a result, when I encountered dissension in my youth, I vanished as quickly as possible. However, now after having seven children, this was no longer true. I became one of the biggest dissenters I know. My lack of courage during that episode in college took a long period of time to ask God to forgive me and to be able to forgive myself.

Another disturbing time was when my dad died from a heart attack. I was not there for him as I should have been. My lack of determination at that time brought me much sorrow. However, I knew God forgave me. He granted me the grace to forgive myself when I was willing to say, "I'm sorry," as Peter did, and not think forgiveness for my actions was impossible, as Judas did.

During past Lenten seasons, when I have asked God to show me people in my life whom I needed to forgive, I have had some amazing revelations. For instance, years ago in an inter-club paddle tennis group, there was a lady who literally could not tolerate me to the point of being rude. We had never had anything to do with one another prior to this commitment, but she simply refused to look at or speak to me. It was not a pleasant situation in which to be involved, but I simply chose to ignore it. I was never one to confront someone, but in trying to simply ignore what was happening it just went into my garbage can for future disposal. God clearly showed me that I had never forgiven the lady and I needed to do so.

Another unexpected "expose" was with a doctor on duty at the Air Force Base Hospital. He decided, when I arrived late one night after having a spontaneous miscarriage, that I had brought this abortion upon myself, or at least this was my interpretation as a result of his obnoxious behavior. When in the midst of hemorrhaging to death, the last thing I wanted was to encounter an unsympathetic physician. It took me a while to realize why he was performing in such a manner. It then occurred to me that I had become very angry as a result. This was another creature on God's earth I had never forgiven. I just chose to ignore the situation, which was not the solution to the problem as God clearly spelled out to me.

When people say to me that they simply can not forgive someone in their lives, I relate to them what a lady once told me as she departed from our airplane after a pilgrimage to China. She exclaimed, "I have forgiven the person who murdered my son!" We were both standing in the aisle of the plane at this time, never really having conversed before, but for some reason she felt called to share this miracle with me. If she could forgive someone under those circumstances, it seemed reasonable that most of us could make peace with our trivial, or not so trivial, grievances.

Likewise, another encounter was with two ladies in a prayer group I previously attended. They both had experienced great tragedies in their lives. I would have never known this to be true when conversing with them, because each one had such a great loving relationship with God. There was no anger or hatred present. They had forgiven. One lady had her 30-year-old son murdered by a hitchhiker whom he picked up one night. She explained that in asking God for her not to harbor unforgiveness, He took it away that night and by morning she felt completely peaceful. The other lady had a daughter murdered by a next-door neighbor while she baby-sat. To make matters worse, two of her sons also died not long after this tragedy. These ladies were such a delight to meet.

God truly heals if we ask Him for the grace to do it. I don't want it any longer, Lord, please take it! "To err is human. To forgive is divine," as Shakespeare said. It is but for us to ask.

"Getting Rid of the Garbage"

In my earlier trips to Medjugorje, I was not favorably impressed by the copious amounts of garbage that littered the countryside. It was mind boggling to me until I realized this was simply an outward sign of inner garbage that people were divesting themselves of before leaving Medjugorje.

In order for us to return home cleansed of all the trash we have been holding onto for years, we must go to confession. We need to empty ourselves of our past and present sins, including unforgiveness of self and others. Fumes of spiritual decay have literally asphyxiated our souls as a result of leaving no room for God.

Confession is big business in Medjugorje, hence the Blessed Mother's name, Mary Queen of Peace. Peace reigns in our hearts when we make room for God instead of garbage. Here it is Lord, take it, I am truly sorry!

A gentleman, whom I met on one of my visits to Medjugorje, mentioned to me that he had not gone to confession in seventeen years. When I encountered him days later, he jubilantly announced that he "did it" and he felt like a new creation.

"The Lost Will be Found"

The Blessed Mother says that the Rosary is the second most powerful prayer after the Mass or the Eucharist. I can certainly attest to seeing miraculous results from reciting the Rosary. On many of my pilgrimages I have witnessed the Blessed Mother's intervention through her favorite prayer. It has brought remarkable results.

We were gathered in Seoul, Korea on a field with 700,000 people in order to celebrate Mass with Pope John Paul II, who was in the country for the Eucharistic Conference. We were with a small group of pilgrims from the Divine Mercy Shrine in Stockbridge, Massachusetts and were scheduled to proceed to Mainland China after a brief visit to Hong Kong. During this time however, the U.S. Government was not encouraging travel to China because of the Tiananmen Square incident which had occurred only months before. Soldiers with machine guns patrolled the streets of Beijing.

Returning to our bus, which was parked a considerable distance away from where we had celebrated Mass, our group leader became aware that one of the elderly Fathers in our group was missing. This priest had had extensive heart surgery several years prior to our trip and could become very confused at times. The thought of him being lost in such a crowd of non-English speaking people was terrifying. As a result, several of us knew we needed Mother Mary's help at that very instant. Miraculously, into our second Rosary we realized "the lost" had been found. God strikes again.

This poor man also disappeared in the Forbidden City in Beijing. In both instances he was missing for a considerable length of time, but true to form, the Rosary brought results. The Shepherd rescued His lamb.

"Dragons in the Sky"

The sky was dark and foreboding in an area of west Texas along highway I-10. The desert with sparsely covered mountains surrounded us as we drove toward El Paso. I noticed underneath the threatening sky a relatively small black cloud shaped like a dragon. I could actually make out its whip-like tail, outstretched claws, and even smoke spewing forth from its mouth.

As I drove behind my husband's car, I was astounded to see his antenna pop off the roof like a cork out of a champagne bottle. The wind had intensified to such an extent that it was impossible for us to stay on the road. As we pulled off the highway, sheets of rain pummeled us for what seemed like an eternity. Although I was parked, due to the driving rain which was streaming parallel to the ground, it gave the sensation that my truck was moving. I sat there with my foot on the brake, and became aware that I was praying in tongues.

Gradually, the wind and rain subsided which allowed us to continue on our way. After a few miles down the road three incredible rainbows side by side greeted us. In addition, a large cloud shaped like an angel floated in the sky nearby. Never before or since have I encountered rainbows as huge or colorful as these.

My husband later remarked to me that he thought my vehicle was going to blow away. I did too! Thank You, Lord. Fortunately, the back of my truck was filled with rosaries, Mary Queen of Peace newspapers, and metal sculptures. All of which, including those prayers, prevented me from disappearing into the "I-10 hinterland."

"How Grateful Can You Get?"

My granddaughter Lisa and I were driving from Ashton, Idaho to Phoenix, Arizona. On the thruway around Salt Lake City, in heavy 4:00 p.m. Sunday traffic, my tire suddenly blew. We were in the passing lane but fortunately were able to immediately move over to the far side of the road and pull off the highway. When we examined the blowout we found a six-inch hole in the left front tire. Doing any further driving was an impossibility. "OK Lisa, let's start saying the Rosary. We need help right now!" As we finished the last Hail Mary, a police car pulled up and, needless to say, we were ecstatic. I told him how happy we were to see him and he replied, "Lady, I haven't heard those words very much today!"

He took great care of us. Maybe this cop was feeling pretty unwanted, understandably so, yet God showed him just how truly needed he was that Sunday afternoon. Can you imagine someone saying to this policeman, who had just been stopped for speeding, "Oh, I'm so happy to see you today? Thank you very much for this lovely ticket. God Bless You." And who knows, he may have saved their life!

"Man in the Brown Suit"

My friend Lou decided after being in Calcutta, India for several days that she could not possibly live any longer without soft toilet tissue or coffee. As we walked along a road not far from Mother Teresa's Motherhouse at 5:30 on a Sunday evening, we encountered a German lady emerging from a long alley who was looking for Mother Teresa's residence. After giving her instructions, Lou inquired if she had seen any open shops on the "street" from which she had just emerged. The lady replied that it was a possibility, since there were small businesses lining the thoroughfare. This was all the encouragement my friend needed.

She took off like a shot down the dark alley. I was bringing up the rear yelling, "Lou, let's spend the night in town and look for your necessities in the morning. It's an insane place to be in the dark." No one would have been caught dead in such an area. There were some bars, a few dark shops, and no sign of life anywhere! Help, God, do something! I was really praying. Lou was absolutely deaf to anything I said. She was on a mission. Then suddenly, out of nowhere, a man appeared who was dressed in a brown suit and cream-colored shirt. He was attired in a peculiar manner for that area of India. He inquired, in perfect English, whether he could be of help to us. Lou explained to him her dilemma, whereby the gentleman took us on our journey. Finally, after traipsing maybe a half-mile down the "street," we found an apothecary shop which was open and had exactly what madam was seeking. Our friend then offered to find us a cab since where we lived was 45 minutes away from town. He was gone only a few minutes before he reappeared announcing that he had found a cab whose driver he knew. He then stated that he would drive with us to our destination. Throughout the trip he did not speak to the driver, to Lou, or to me until I asked him what he did for a living. He responded that he was in "part-time security." I mulled that one over and came to the conclusion that he was either a communist policeman or an angel.

All of a sudden Lou exclaimed that she did not recognize any of our surroundings, whereby fear washed over me like ocean waves. We were going to be raped! We were going to die! No, I trust You, Lord! These thoughts repeated themselves over and over in my head until we finally recognized where we were. Thank You, Lord!

That night she desperately needed to go to the bathroom; therefore, she did not wish to hassle with the cab driver over our fare. She simply paid him more than she felt was warranted, telling him to give something to his companion in the front seat. The "security agent" simply said, "He won't give me anything!" During the entire drive they never spoke to one another. This was odd, since he had said he knew the cab driver. He simply sat royally in the front seat of the car.

A short time later we related our experience to one of the nuns, who excitedly exclaimed, "Haven't you ever heard the story of the angel in the brown suit?"

In addition, one of the sisters in town who was familiar with the area near the Motherhouse later told us that she would not have been caught dead in that alley. Drug transactions, prostitution, etc. were reasons enough to avoid it all cost.

God saved two screwy ladies who obviously were not able to save themselves. Thank You for sending us an Angel, Lord!

"*You Can't Please Them All*"

Father was the type of individual who was always busy, just like most of us can be. One morning I approached him after the Church service to speak with him for a few minutes. I was told that it was not possible because he had too much on his agenda for the day. His response definitely pushed one of my buttons. As a result, I came forth with, "Well, Father, I hope that God has the time, when you die!" He told me later that I was his conscience that morning.

He also told me that he was being transferred out of our parish and was in the process of trying to locate a replacement. He stated, "God Himself could not please these people."

We all know that God Himself pleases very few people. We are too busy wanting to be God. If God cannot please all, how can we possibly expect to?

"Never Say No"

One day I received a phone call from my daughter in Louisiana saying that Mother Teresa was going to be in Lafayette the day I was to arrive in New Orleans. If we stopped very briefly at her home in Donaldsonville after picking me up at the airport, there was a good possibility we could make her appearance three hours later.

The week before my departure, I was praying the Stations of the Cross at my Parish Church in Connecticut when I received the message that I was to make a red, white, and blue rosary for Mother Teresa. She was to use these beads to pray for the United States. Why pray for the U.S., Lord?

This incident occurred in the mid-80s when issues other than abortion were not as blatantly obvious as they are today. At this particular time in my life I was making rosaries from those recycled beads, which I spoke of previously. As it was, there were some very subtle red, natural, and blue wooden beads available in my collection. My husband also made a wonderful wooden cross, hence, Mother Teresa's rosary.

Fortunately, Carol and I arrived in Lafayette in time for Mother Teresa's appearance, but unfortunately not near enough to find a seat facing the stage. We positioned ourselves behind the speaker's platform since nothing else was available. We had a great rear view of the entire evening's performance. The only problem was that the acoustics were so poor in this part of the auditorium that I could not understand a word that Mother Teresa said. As a result, I simply spent the time praying.

As the program came to a close there was an announcement that Mother Teresa would not be able to see anyone because her plane departed immediately. I then grabbed a policeman (the place was crawling with security agents) and asked him if he knew how I could get the rosary to her before she left. He replied that it was not possible unless I wished to give it to the Bishop who could then possibly give it to Mother Teresa.

We ran looking for a rather small obscure door and garage entrance which would indicate where the saintly lady might emerge. We stepped through the door and entered a room, which was teamed with security agents. A van had its motor running. Two of Mother's nuns were barely visible in the front seat of the vehicle, but obviously Mother Teresa was somewhere within. I knew I had to give it my best effort to get the rosary to Mother Teresa. As a result, I started to pound on the window by the driver's seat. In desperation the nun opened up the window to see what could possibly be the problem. I explained to her that I had a rosary for Mother which was to be used to pray for the U.S. She turned toward the back of the van from where Mother no doubt gave her consent to accept it. Unbelievably, it did not appear that any of the policeman noticed what we were doing. It was like we did not exist. As we started to leave we noticed that there was a knock on the outside door to which an agent responded but refused entrance to a lady who was also seeking access to the area.

Seemingly unnoticed, we exited from the building only to be greeted by a magnificent rainbow in the Western sky. There was no sign of rain in our surroundings, but at dusk once more, we encountered a glorious rainbow traversing the highway as we headed home. The next day on the way to Mass I beheld yet another rainbow in the morning sky! Too much, Lord!

Nothing is impossible with God as He clearly showed us in Lafayette that evening. His angels can make us invisible, if it is His will and you are ready to say "yes."

"Angels in the Night"

My sister-in-law in Annapolis was bedridden in the final stages of cancer. My brother had asked me to please come and spend a few days with him as often as possible for emotional support. There were only the two of us left in the immediate family.

One Saturday evening at 11:30, my brother and I chatted in the kitchen. After a short time, we decided to adjourn to our bedrooms. After getting myself dressed for the night, I went into the living room for my prayer time, when I suddenly heard a tremendous crash on the road in front of the house. As I continued to pray, not knowing exactly what action should be taken, there was a loud tapping on the window. I checked to see whom could it be when I saw a neighbor running across the lawn yelling, "Bring a blanket somebody, quick!" The house sat back a considerable distance from the highway, so other than a few visible lights through the trees it was not possible to observe what had happened on the dark road. I grabbed a blanket and my bathrobe and headed out to the street.

There in the driveway lay an unconscious young male bleeding profusely from his nose. Bodies were strewn about on the highway, but my job seemed to be to pray for this young boy. Consequently, I knelt beside him speaking to him intermittently between my prayers to let him know that he was O.K. I kept telling him that he was O.K. and he was fine. It was most important that I assured him of his well-being. I am convinced that when people are unconscious they can hear what is going on but physically cannot respond. Soon, the medics and police arrived but no one disturbed me as I knelt beside him fervently praying. It was almost like I wasn't there. They had called for a helicopter from the trauma unit in Baltimore; however, it was in use somewhere else. While continuing to pray, I heard a man who was standing nearby say, "It's no use, he's dead," which he continually repeated. As a result, I became very angry at his remarks and told him to please stop saying it. Afterwards when I talked to this gentleman, he shared with me that his wife had died of cancer just three months before.

All of the victims were naturally very shaken by what had taken place. The man, whose wife had died, talked freely about his loss. When the helicopter finally arrived it was too late, the young man had died. However, it did not seem to matter when I prayed for him whether he lived or died. He just needed to know that he was fine. The hospice ladies who took care of my sister-in-law were familiar with the young males that were involved in the crash. Apparently, they were in a hurry to meet their midnight curfew, and impudently passed other cars, causing a head-on collision.

I knew that night had a definite purpose in many people's lives. For instance, my sister-in-law had much to think about besides her own death. She had another soul to pray for. The man whose wife had died three months prior, seemed to have a great need to share his experience of his wife's fatal illness. It may have been extremely heal-ing for him to know that in our home we were likewise into the throes of a loved one's impending death. My sister-in-law died ten days later.

Afterwards, I spoke to the mother of the boy who had died in the accident. I was able to tell her that he passed away very peacefully, never regaining consciousness, and that God allowed me to pray over him for a long time. She shared with me that his sixteen-year-old cousin had died six months before this incident under similar circumstances. They were very close friends. She was pleased that there was someone there for her son that night.

The angels truly allowed me to be invisible to the medics who surrounded this young male. They never asked me to move from my kneeling position, nor spoke to me, or even acknowledged my presence in any way. God is good. He is generous with his angels and His love for each and every one of us.